Dr Marny Lishman is the author of *Burnout to Brilliant*, as well as a health and community psychologist, wellbeing and mindset coach, keynote speaker and media commentator. A sought-after national mental health and wellbeing expert, she provides commentary on a variety of mental health topics on TV, radio and in print.

Crisis
to
Contentment

DR MARNY LISHMAN, PSYCHOLOGIST

affirm
press

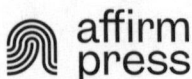

affirm press

First published by Affirm Press in 2025
Bunurong/Boon Wurrung Country
28 Thistlethwaite Street
South Melbourne VIC 3205
affirmpress.com.au

10 9 8 7 6 5 4 3 2 1

Affirm Press is located on the unceded land of the Bunurong/Boon Wurrung peoples of the Kulin Nation. Affirm Press pays respect to their Elders past and present.

A catalogue record for this book is available from the National Library of Australia

ISBN: 9781923135093 (paperback)

Cover design by Alissa Dinallo © Affirm Press
Author image by Donna Fortune Photography
Typeset in 11/16.5 pt Adobe Text Pro by Post Pre-press Group, Brisbane
Proudly printed and bound in Australia by the Opus Group

While this is a work of nonfiction, some names and identifying details have been changed to protect the privacy of the people involved.

This book does not constitute individual psychological advice as everyone's needs are different. If you are in crisis, please reach out to a mental health professional.

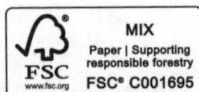

MIX
Paper | Supporting responsible forestry
FSC® C001695

To my Fellow Wise Midlifers,
May we keep learning, loving & laughing.
xx

'Ageing is an extraordinary process whereby you become the person you always should have been.'
David Bowie

Contents

Introduction

IN 2016, THEN-44-YEAR-OLD Hollywood actor Ben Affleck was photographed standing alone outside a building in London. Clad in a blue jumper, dark denim jeans and blue sneakers, and with a salt-and-pepper unshaven beard, the reluctantly famous actor was snapped with a cigarette in hand, head tilted up, eyes closed, inhaling deeply and looking ... desperately irritated. Whether he was frustrated at being caught having a sneaky ciggie on a break, was having a mindful moment in the fresh air, was just a little stressed or had removed himself from a situation that had left him fervently annoyed, we will never know. But whatever the reason, I for one have never resonated more with a photo.

Grumpy Ben Affleck looks like how I've been feeling lately, and given it's become an internet meme in recent years, it seems others have been feeling similarly. Memes only gain traction if they resonate. The photo encapsulates that feeling of having to bite your tongue, remove yourself from a situation, close your eyes, gather your thoughts and just ... breathe. The chain reaction that leads to this moment usually starts off with a rough baseline feeling of exhaustion, followed by a gradual rising of annoyance in reaction to a situation at hand, then a realisation that we probably can't say what we really want to say out loud (likely because it's socially inappropriate), so we just slink away to be alone for a bit. We then return once we're back to some sort of emotional homeostasis and can tackle the situation with a sound mind.

Now, I don't smoke and nor am I a man, but in the last couple of years I've noticed that I've felt like Grumpy Ben Affleck more than ever. The irritation has increased, the tolerance has decreased and the eye-rolling has quadrupled (in real life and in emoji format). I've seriously wondered whether I'm morphing (metaphorically speaking) into a grumpy middle-aged man. Now, don't get me wrong – I know and love many grumpy middle-aged men. This is not meant as an insult. It's just that I've been observing some subtle and not-so-subtle similarities in the way I, as a woman, have been feeling, thinking and behaving lately that remind me of the irritated yet wise male midlifers I've worked with or grown up with. I'm a self-aware and introspective person (one would hope, given I'm a psychologist) so all this has had me thinking. Given the trials and tribulations of my life so far, which I've navigated reasonably well, why does this particular moment feel a little tougher? Surely I've been through harder moments before. What on earth is going on with me? What's changed? Why has this pervasive irritation slowly crept up on me? Why do I just want to just run away and spend more time alone? Why am I feeling unhappy about things that used to make me feel happy? Why do I feel more anxiety than I've ever felt? Why don't I want to have conversations about trivial things anymore? Why am I so disappointed with humanity when I watch the news? Why do I feel so tired? Why am I getting a bit panicky that the years are moving by so quickly? Are other people my age feeling like this? Is this going to continue? Am I destined to live in a cabin in a forest with 30 cats? And, come to think of it, why does that sound so appealing?

Naturally, as these thoughts came to me, I started going a bit deeper. When things go a little bit awry, I tend to go internal first to try to figure things out for myself. Perhaps it's just me getting older, or that I'm not going to bed early enough. Maybe I have too much on my plate and I'm a bit stressed and overwhelmed with the sheer amount of stuff that needs to get done. Have I been spending too much time by myself, so that people just annoy me in general now? Is it my declining oestrogen and progesterone? That I'm out of alignment somewhere in my career? Should I be dating more? Am I not drinking enough water? Did I just forget to take my vitamin B?

Failing to find any satisfying answers, I endeavoured to search wider, wondering what external factors could be contributing to my shift in mood. Is there anything else that could be contributing to my descent into doom and gloom with a dash of anxiety? Is there something going on my life that I'm worried about? Are there specific people I spend time with who are particularly irritating? Is the world going to pot and I'm just reacting to that? Have I watched too many TikTok doomsday videos? Do I have a 'pandemic hangover'? Did Mercury retrograde and get stuck there? Are there actually just more people out there who rightly deserve my silent, passive annoyance? I knew something was going on.

And then, at the peak of my pondering on the causes of my Grumpy Ben Affleck metamorphosis, I stumbled on an article about midlife entitled, 'Forty-seven is the saddest age of all, study finds: "There is an unhappiness curve"'. Then this: '"Middle age misery" peaks at 47.2 years of age – but do the statistics ring true?' And then it hit me. It's a thing! Many people in their 40s are feeling like this. It's universal: adults in midlife are likely to be feeling tired, miserable, confused and a tad annoyed. It's middle age. It's simply that. Phew. I could do something with that.

I'm middle-aged. Around 47.2. Ripe, mature and well into adulthood. Perhaps smack in the middle – if I'm lucky – of my life. I've lived my first half, and now I'm tipping over into the second half. I'm slightly nervous about not knowing whether these invisible life halves will be equal in length, or if the second half will rip me off and be cut short.

I'm not in denial of my age (well, maybe a little), nor embarrassed. I've just been busy doing other things and failed to notice that I've moved into the midlife age bracket. I hadn't yet thought of myself as middle-aged. Middle age was reserved for many of my clients, my parents and their friends, my bosses in previous jobs, my university lecturers, my doctors, politicians I had voted for, game-show hosts and the couple that owns my favourite Italian restaurant down the road. Yes, I've noticed that people such as my parents have gone from middle-aged to elderly in the last decade, but I neglected to see that I was creeping up behind them, slipping into the middle-age position they just left.

Yes, come to think of it, the signs of middle age have been there for a while. I have a 'special' chair I like to sit on in the lounge room, I pick the plain vanilla flavour at the ice-cream shop, I know the exact time of year I need to prune my roses, I save plant clippings in little jars, I internally sigh when people ask me to go out in the evenings, I love nothing more than walking around old bookstores and I have a strong urge to move to a quiet and remote coastal town where nothing happens.

Middle age is the cluster of years halfway between our childhood and old age. The exact range is up for debate – and with eternal youth seemingly on everyone's agenda, I can imagine it will continue to be – but at present, it describes the period between 40 and around 60 years of age. With advances in medical technology (and moisturiser) many would disagree, saying that these days the middle-age years could be stretched out well into our 70s. Some people class themselves as middle-aged in their 30s, while others reject the idea for as long as they can and don't identify with this term until they're well over 60. Of course, to add to the confusion, on top of our biological age, we also have a subjective age, which is determined by how we *feel* in body and mind. I was describing the concoction of grumpy emotions I've been feeling of late to a younger male friend of mine, and he resonated straight away, saying, 'I feel like that now' – he is only 35. So perhaps the unhappiest age may or may not be 47.2 exactly but stretched out around ten years or so either side, all depending on how we are feeling, physically and mentally, at the time. We can argue all day about what chunk of our life is classed as midlife. It doesn't matter. We're unlikely to be walking around calling ourselves middle-aged and might even, like myself, be in subconscious denial of it. But I think it's a helpful discussion to have given so many of us have been feeling a little 'off' lately.

Midlife, middle age or, if we believe the birthday cards our friends satirically gift us once we crack the big 4-0, 'over the hill': it all sounds a bit vanilla, really, a bit mature, a bit like all the excitement in life is behind us. The 'prime of our life' sounds a bit more exciting, as does 'midlife renaissance' or, if we want to sexy it up a little more, 'milieu de vie'. Everything sounds better in French.

In this period that we call middle age, however long it may be, there are a lot of changes. Like a *lot*. And these changes can cause us some angst. I've seen this phenomenon often over the years, in my clients, my mother, my friends and now myself. Even social media is awash with conversations explaining the changes that occur in midlife.

Or complaining about them.

And all these changes are happening at the time in our lives when we seem to be most under the pump *and* when our mental load is at its peak. We wear multiple hats and are in multiple roles, often not having much of a village to share the overflow. We're part of the sandwich generation, with elderly parents to look after but simultaneously with kids who need us to pick them up from school and to make sure they're at football practice on time. We're often at the peak of our careers (and trying to figure out if we still *like* the career we naively chose 20 years ago). And, of course, we're trying to get up at 5am for sunrise yoga because that's what the 20-year-old influencer told us we need to be doing to look as healthy, happy and successful as them.

We're living in a fast-paced modern world that is exponentially advancing at a rate our human brains can't keep up with. On the other hand, humanity seems to be going backwards with heartbreaking global crisis after crisis, which we're helplessly watching play out in real time on devices glued to our fingertips.

Whether it's body changes, career changes, children getting older, caring for elderly parents, dealing with the loss of loved ones, relationship changes, friendship changes or keeping up with the fast-paced societal changes that we never seem to be ready for (or all the above), as the current generation of midlifers we have a lot on our plates. We're trying to be wise, be cool, be healthy and be accepting of the fact that our bodies are changing. (It's a thudding realisation, as a woman especially, when you move to brush a white hair off your cheek but realise the hair isn't *on* your cheek, but rather growing out of it.)

But excitingly, yes, there's some good stuff that happens during this period! And I welcome it. I've spent a lot of time working with people who have journeyed through middle age and have heard about the difficult transformation that they too encountered during these years. With hindsight, many report that the internal struggle of middle age is just what they needed. They realise they wouldn't be where they are now without it; that the middle-age havoc and ambivalence of mind while navigating myriad internal and external changes needed to happen. Tapping into the wisdom acquired during the middle-age journey has led them to refine their lives. They needed to change their ways, they needed their life to change, they needed the push to head in a different direction. Life needed to get better. And it did.

Middle age can be a deeply evaluative time. For many midlifers, this is the opportunity to hop off the socially constructed pathway they were thrust on in their early years and start laying one that is more aligned with who they truly are. The midlife years can be a beneficial transformation, not something to fear. It's a time that may elicit a host of negative feelings (just ask Ben Affleck), but these might be telling us something about ourselves and our lives. With deep reflection, we can tap into the learnings from our first half of life and apply them to the second half. Life can get better than it ever was before. As David Bowie once said, 'Ageing is an extraordinary process whereby you become the person you always should have been.'

In this book, we'll take a journey through the various crises that us middle-agers might experience, no matter how uncomfortable, irritating or even inconvenient they may be, and learn about the changes we can make which can propel us in the direction of contentment. We kick things off in Part 1 by talking about why crisis is inevitable in life but disaster isn't. We'll explore what a crisis is, different types of crisis (and crises) that we may go through across our lifespan – specifically the crises experienced by our generation (yes, awesome gen Xers and older millennials, I'm talking to you!). We then discuss how the wisdom we gain from crises can benefit us as we continue our life journey. Part 2 covers many different areas of life where we may find ourselves a little stuck, full of annoyance or even feeling a little confused about it all. We will cover a host of crises and changes that us middle-agers might stumble on including emotions, thinking, physical health, relationships, family, solitude, friendship, work life, hobbies, grief, inner peace, global upheavals and even reconciling with the past. At the end of each chapter in Part 2 I ask you to reflect on your own experience with a 'Considerations' section; I 'Challenge' you with an activity that may help move you to contentment; and I ask for your 'Commitment' to ritualise something you may have learned during the chapter. And then, in Part 3 I present you with a Midlife Review (I have to give you homework – I'm a psychologist!) which gives you the chance to wrap up everything you have learned through the whole book and focus on what you specifically want to work on to move from crisis to contentment.

So, whether you're already annoyed in your 20s, you've had enough of everyone by your 50s or you're feeling a bit WTF about life in the years in between, this book is for you. While we might not all go through a stereotypical midlife crisis we are all vulnerable to mini crises on the bumpy road towards our mature adulthood years. These moments might render us a bit stuck, a bit blue and a bit grumpy at times, but there's wisdom that can be found in each of them if we just think about them a little deeper. We can use that wisdom to build a beautiful life of serenity, fulfilment and clarity.

PART 1

Crisis Is Inevitable, But Disaster Isn't

CHAPTER 1

What Is a Crisis?

IN MARCH 2020, Australians were glued to our television sets watching news anchors report global Covid-19 infection rates (and deaths), which were rising before our eyes. We were anxiously waiting for our state leaders to give us orders as to whether we were to stay inside, wear masks, take our kids to school or go to work, while we saw harrowing footage of chaos in overseas hospitals. Media commentators (including me) were discussing the pandemic and its impacts on TV and radio, as well as writing opinion pieces, giving a voice to how the public was feeling and providing some expertise to explain why people were behaving like they had all of a sudden been plunged into doomsday pandemonium.

As the fear and lack of control in our lives persisted, guidance on what to do next remained scarce and feelings of disconnection increased. Stress levels in our society were skyrocketing. We blamed everyone we could for how we were feeling: our premiers, our prime minister, our partners ... pangolins. Chaos ensued, not only in the outside world and in our homes but also in our minds. While scientists and medical experts from around the world were scrambling to find a solution or a cure or a treatment for this deadly new virus, us psychologists were working with our clients, busier than we had ever been. We worked through the acute 'pandemic' of stress that had exacerbated people's pre-existing issues. But at the same time, we were quietly observing a society in crisis, thinking to ourselves, 'We ain't seen nothing yet ...' We were heading for a mental health crisis.

The Covid-19 pandemic continues to impact the world. It's been one of the most significant crises of modern times and has resulted in millions of deaths, overwhelmed healthcare systems, disrupted economies and widespread social and psychological effects. Psychologically we're still in the early days of coming through the crisis – some are even calling this phenomenon a 'pandemic hangover'.

Whenever we think of global crises, we associate with them the perceived negative emotions of those who experience them. These are emotions that many of us try to steer away from or even deny: overwhelm, anxiety, agitation, fear, anger, confusion, helplessness and sometimes hopelessness. It's a hodgepodge of feelings that all sound rather dreadful. Rarely are the more positive emotions associated with the word 'crisis'. It's considered something to avoid at all costs, something that nothing good can come from. We should just steer clear.

There are different ways to define a crisis, depending on who you ask. Historians and politicians often describe crisis as a period of conflict or instability. Think the Cuban Missile Crisis or the Global Financial Crisis. The word 'crisis' literally means 'a time of intense difficulty or danger' or 'a time when a difficult or important decision must be made'. But in health literature, it is defined as 'the turning point of a disease when an important change takes place, indicating either recovery or death' – you can see that the meaning diverges.

For our purposes, we can come up with our own definition: a crisis is a period of change or instability that, given our psychological capabilities, we may find tough to navigate, but that can be a catalyst for something better. To quote Shakespeare, 'The web of our life is of a mingled yarn, good and ill together.' Crises might be global or local; they might be collective or individual; they might be big or small. Crises will happen to other people but, yes, they will also happen to us. Unfortunately, no matter how hard we try to avoid moments of crisis in our own lives, they can be imposed on us, and we will be forced to navigate them whether we want to or not.

Emotions experienced during a crisis can vary widely depending on the nature of the crisis, our individual circumstances and the coping mechanisms we have in our psychological repertoire. Using the pandemic as an example, people's feelings, thoughts and behaviours were all wildly different, dependent on so many variables. Some of us were having the time of our lives working from home in our activewear, while others were disconnected and in a state of despair. Some of us rode the disruption unfazed, while others practically stampeded through shopping centres, knocking people over to fill their trolleys with toilet paper.

People naturally get bogged down in the negative emotions of a crisis, but among the panic and confusion, they can be a turning point. The power lies in going through them, riding the waves of them. They can give us new perspectives on life and, as a bonus, give us the internal capabilities and coping strategies to deal with future crises, inoculating us against the inevitable difficult times to come and fostering within us a wisdom that can be imparted onto others. We will always resist a crisis at first when we see it coming – that's natural – but there are some that will sneak up on us whether we are ready for them or not. That's life.

CHAPTER 2

Life Stages and Their Crises

BACK IN THE late 1980s I remember going to the cinema to see a Saturday movie with my mother. It was called *Shirley Valentine* and was a tale that followed the life of the titular Shirley, a middle-aged housewife from Liverpool who finds herself stuck in a monotonous life. Feeling unfulfilled, rather dull and confined by societal expectations of her as a woman, she embarks on a journey of self-discovery when she takes a spontaneous trip with a girlfriend to Greece. Amid the idyllic Mediterranean setting, this middle-aged woman rediscovers her zest for life, her long-lost passion and, importantly, her freedom. Through her humorous and poignant encounters with the locals (including an energetic but short-lived fling with the very smooth Costas Dimitriades) Shirley learns to embrace her true self, breaking free from the shackles of her past and becoming excited about the possibilities of her future.

This movie resonated with midlifers (women in particular, but I'm sure many men dragged to the cinema would have received a bit of a wake-up call too) around the globe back then, spurring a sellout run of the one-woman play the film was based on. Shirley's empowering story reflected to women something they saw in themselves but would likely never admit. That at midlife, adults can still be deeply confused about life, wondering what it's all about, wondering how they became so out of alignment and thinking that something must change. But they just don't know what or how ... yet. This movie held a mirror up to millions of midlifers.

I found the movie entertaining but didn't relate to it, being an egocentric 12- or 13-year-old at the time and more interested in what Johnny Depp and Rob Lowe were up to. But I do recall absorbing the lessons about what I *didn't* want my life to look like when I became middle-aged: being trapped in a relationship I didn't want to be in, living a humdrum life with a monotonous, unfulfilling job, being taken for granted by my children, feeling invisible to those around me and having no one but the kitchen wall to impart my wisdom onto, as Shirley did daily. 'Hello, wall,' she would say as she prepared her husband's nightly 'egg and chip' dinner in the kitchen. If it hadn't had an impact on my psyche at some level, I probably wouldn't be writing about it now, over 30 years later, and it would be long-lost in the catalogue of 80s movies I consumed so long ago. This movie put the fear of midlife angst, mediocrity and invisibility into me. Thinking about midlife crisis so early probably set me up well for the one that was to hit me (or at least firmly tap me on the shoulder).

The first individual 'crisis' we tend to encounter, all things having gone well prior, is the adolescent identity crisis. This is when teenagers are trying to figure out who they are while their brains and bodies are changing at a rapid rate. Contrary to what many parents of teenagers may think (i.e. that nothing *at all* is going on in their minds), there is so much growth happening in their brains while they unconsciously work out their place in the world. Many of us look back at photos of our teenage years and wonder what on earth we were thinking at the time, like why we ever thought a perm was a good idea. It was a time of being curious about the world but also being heavily influenced by it. It was a time of trying new things, working out our values (or compromising them), testing out the beliefs we'd grown up with and trying to create a future for ourselves. And then basically seeing what stuck. It was a tough time, but if you're reading this, you got through it and emerged out the other side into adulthood.

Then a decade or so later, once we've had a good crack at our younger years, along might come the quarter-life crisis. In our mid-20s to early 30s, we may start feeling uncertain, disillusioned and anxious, questioning our life choices thus far. We can become deeply reflective, asking ourselves, what's working? What isn't? We might think about what needs to happen for us to get back on track or move ourselves onto a better path. This crisis often arises from societal pressure to establish a stable career, find meaningful relationships and achieve personal goals, all while we're grappling with the realities of adulthood. This crisis, though, allows us a course-correction of sorts.

Then a decade (or two) later we may have the midlife crisis. This is a period of emotional turmoil that can see middle-aged adults grapple with many changes in themselves, their roles in society and the world around them. The midlife crisis has various negative connotations, such as the sudden desire to buy a red sports car, leave a long-term relationship or other drastic measure to alleviate the unwelcomed angst. But these changes, expected and unexpected, can also involve a lot of reflecting and questioning, all of which can help redirect adults in a more positive direction in the next chapters of their lives. It can be a more mindful and purposeful experience for adults to live through, and hence the focus of this book.

Later (a lot later), in old age, we may confront a developmental end-of-life crisis characterised by reflection and possibly acceptance of, and even preparation for, death. This crisis may involve reconciling past regrets, finding meaning and closure, and making decisions about legacy and end-of-life care. We may ask ourselves whether we lived well and whether there's anything else left for us to do – a psychological tying of loose ends. In reflecting on their own mortality, some of my older clients start back-pedalling after hitting a cluster of emotions that they didn't expect. As they transition from a career and family focused life into retirement, many of them unexpectedly hit crisis point, experiencing feelings of uncertainty, loss of purpose and boredom. Some of them reject what society says they should be doing at this late age and go back to work.

Sometimes life crises are dealt with consciously, but usually they occur unconsciously, meaning that for the most part, they might manifest as a feeling of dissatisfaction that we can't pinpoint. There may or may not be a specific reason we can identify for the low mood, disappointment or panic that sets in as we slide closer to the next big birthday. We might feel angst but not know why. These feelings can be somewhat confusing, particularly when they're out of character (as I discovered).

Sometimes life crises are triggered because we thought we would have achieved A, B and C by a certain age and anxiety sets in, along with a large glass of despair, when we haven't. Often we look around at others in our cohort, unhelpfully compare ourselves to them and get hung up on what 'should' be happening by a particular life stage: the perfect career, marriage, kids, fancy house, money, flash car, overseas holidays ... If we haven't ticked these things off by a prescribed age, a feeling of uneasiness may creep in.

The articles I found when I was morphing into an uncharacteristic grumpy pants for no apparent reason mentioned that the unhappiest age was on average 47.2 in developed countries (and 48.2 in developing countries). This was based on research by Dartmouth professor

David Blanchflower, who had studied humans in over 132 countries and found that everyone, regardless of location and economic wellbeing, experiences a U-shaped happiness curve, hitting their lowest point in their late 40s. (The good news is that things tend to get better after that.) Despite some saying that the midlife crisis might be a myth, it's clear that us midlifers are going through some serious psychological anguish during this time period.

Psychoanalyst Elliott Jaques coined the term 'midlife crisis' in the 1960s after observing that individuals in their midlife often experienced a period of depression and abrupt lifestyle changes as they grappled with the concept of mortality. For many of us, the term evokes the stereotypical image of a middle-aged man with a new red Porsche (or younger girlfriend), a time of insecurity that leads to extravagant purchases and impulsive decisions in an attempt to soothe one's inner turmoil. But this stereotype oversimplifies the deeper goings-on in midlifers' minds and ignores the fact that even those of us (of any gender) who can't quite afford a Porsche can feel this way, too. Yes, signs of a midlife crisis may include indulgent behaviour (I may even upgrade my Kia – wild, I know ...) but even more common are restlessness and regret for previous decisions, along with nostalgia for past experiences and daydreaming about alternative future paths. While midlife crisis may not be an inevitable reality for everyone, it is for many people, in some shape or form.

Middle age is a chapter in life that was revered in the past but seems to glide by unannounced and without the accolades it deserves in modern times. For much of human history, life expectancy was much lower than it is today, with many individuals not surviving past childhood or early adulthood. Reaching middle age was considered a notable achievement and often marked a transition to a more stable and prosperous period of life. Journalist Patricia Cohen explains in her book *In Our Prime* that the midlife period has historically been characterised by increased responsibility, status and influence within the community. Middle-agers even set the style of fashion in society. They often occupied more established and influential positions, socially and professionally, and younger generations aspired to emulate their choices of attire and grooming. Middle-agers were the trendsetters. In recent times, given our unhealthy obsession with staying young and a skew towards young people being the ones to influence, persuade and advise us, the wisdom once rightly earned by elders has started to lose its value. I even find myself lured, against my better judgement, into taking advice from a bouncy 20-something on social media who might know a lot about herself but without the broader knowledge that only comes with living and ageing.

I'm not alone in this inner battle, in which middle-aged adults are trying to find where they fit in the world where the respect once afforded to those in middle age seems to have eroded. I've had many conversations with people over the years who feel that they are in a sort of limbo, treading the choppy waters between youth and old age. When teenagers go through the trials of adolescence, they usually don't understand that they are going through a necessarily ego-driven transitional period that is crucial for their development; they are just feeling their way through it (and sometimes being a total pain in the arse as a result). You can see them tussle with it for months, sometimes years, being a bit of this and that, rebelling against what they are told to do, until they eventually settle and start moving on a pathway that might be driven somewhat by what they want. I think we feel we have enough free will to head in any direction we want but forget that in many cases we've been unconsciously conditioned to do what society tells us to do, and we deny ourselves the reflection time that would help us tap into what we truly want for our life.

This is why midlife can be so exciting: it's a chance to evaluate what's working and what we still want to try, and the panic of having only half our life left can motivate us to get things done quicker. Although it can be a confusing time, our questioning can be the catalyst for a powerful pivot in a better direction. We start reflecting, asking ourselves: what are my values? What are my beliefs? Am I fulfilled? Have I achieved the goals that I set for myself? Am I living the life I truly want to live? And the big one ... Who am I? How cool is it to have a chance to figure it all out and consciously create what's next for us, and then live it! I too want to have the chance to be a pain in the arse again for a while.

Depending on our individual circumstances and outlook, middle age can be a time of stress, fear and confusion *and* one of stability, growth and contentment. One of my clients, who reluctantly became divorced, found himself made redundant twice, was diagnosed with a chronic disease, put on 20 kilos, broke up with his long-term girlfriend and had to move back in with his parents all in his 40s, said to me, 'My 40s were the shittest decade of my life. I'm about to turn 50 next week, and I'm quite looking forward to it.'

CHAPTER 3

Crisis of a Generation

OVER THE PAST couple of years, I've been struggling with jeans. Having been a denim girl my whole life, this has come as quite a surprise to me. Lately, as I slip my jeans on in the morning with some heels and red lippy, I look in the mirror and think, 'Ugh'. It's a psychological struggle more than anything, because physically they fit (most days). But something's not right. Something has changed.

I'd been happily going about my business for many years, joyously wearing on-trend skinny jeans wherever I go, and now someone (presumably younger than me) has declared that they are no longer in style. I think many women would concur with me that skinny jeans were working quite well for us. We found our skinnies comfortable and flattering. We could wear them casually or dress them up; with a crisp shirt and tailored jacket, they could look so effortlessly polished. Importantly, any shoes went with this style of jeans: long boots, ankle boots, pumps, flats, wedges and sneakers.

But now the jeans that I know and love are supposedly passé, and my perception of myself in the mirror has changed. Being the fashion victim that I am, one day I tossed my black skinnies to the bottom shelf in my wardrobe where all my old jeans go to die and took off to the shops to buy some new ones. I stocked up with a pile of 'in style' denim (determined by who knows who) and reluctantly headed to the horrifyingly lit change rooms.

I began my downward spiral into psychological insecurity with the 'boyfriend' jeans. I didn't mind them too much, but then I made the mistake of looking at the posters above me to see how cool and effortless the teenage models looked in them with their little white singlets and realised I would need to put in a lot of effort to look that cool in them, so I put those jeans back. Then I slipped on the bootleg jeans, but they took me back to Saturday nights in the 90s, drinking Midori and dancing to 'My Sharona' at some grungy nightclub, and I just didn't feel right. Then I tried on some flares, which looked quite nice, but I was sensibly concerned about tripping up in them, so they were a pass, too. Lastly, I tested the 'mom jeans': there was far too much room for me to move in the denim and I felt saggy and scruffy in them. People might think I'd not even tried at all if I bought those. It all felt too hard and I didn't leave with anything. I headed home, pulled my trusted black skinnies off denim death row and felt physically comfortable again. But I was still not feeling right psychologically, fearing that I looked a little like Gru from *Despicable Me*. Although this was a trivial concern in the grand scheme of things, it belied a very real question I was facing: who am I?

Many of us who identify as middle-aged in the present day are generation Xers and older millennials. We're a special sort of middle age, if I don't mind saying so myself. Born in the late 60s, 70s and early 80s – the good old days of big hair, big shoulder pads and big dreams – we took typing classes in high school, worked without computers on our desks, wore tie-dyed shirts, shared our secrets with friends on a telephone attached to the kitchen wall and rode our bikes outside all day long without a skerrick of care. We are also the only generations who have listened to music on vinyl records, tape cassettes, CDs, iPods, iPhones *and* streaming services, and will likely still be around when we're eventually listening to music via implants in our brains. It's an interesting group to be a part of in the world we currently live in. We've got a lot of life under our belts and a lot of life coming up, but right now we're trying to figure out (and keep up with) what's going on in between.

There are so many new things that people who are currently midlife must deal with. Middle age today is different to middle age a century ago; in fact, middle age now feels different than it was even 20 years ago. With advances in healthcare, nutrition and sanitation, people today are living longer than ever before. The middle-age psyche has evolved due to shifts in societal norms, cultural values and economic conditions. There have also been significant changes in gender roles and expectations, particularly regarding women's participation in the workforce, education and leadership roles. Women are more involved in all areas of life, with more power than we have ever had in modern history. But it's also a lot to keep up with. Being the children of baby boomers and earlier generations, who were somewhat restricted in their life options given the global crises that they were raised in, women of our generation were fed a particular ideal. Many of us were weaned on the idea of having it all and are now feeling exhausted as a result. Some areas of society didn't seem to get the full memo that said, yeah, you can be anything you want, you can work hard to get it all ... but you will need some more support. Someone must have ripped that bit off.

Perhaps the inevitable downside of having more choices and roles is that we have more to do. But the upside of more choices is more questions we can ask ourselves. If you hadn't already noticed this about me, I like questions. And could there be a bigger question than 'Who am I?' I can assure you that not many people ask themselves that question, and middle age is a good time to start. We don't have to be what our ancestors at middle age had to be. We don't have to be what we were socially prescribed to be. We have choices. We have time to figure it out. And when we do figure it out, we can change our minds at our discretion. Who we are today is not who we may be tomorrow. This is modern middle age.

Modern middle age also involves us moving with a fast-paced world, trying to exist symbiotically with rapid technological advancements and ever-changing social media trends. We're trying to figure out if that photo was taken by a real person or constructed by AI (while also remembering that we did quite fine without all of these things a few decades ago). And while this all can be a little confusing, it's small compared to some of the bigger issues on our minds. Generation X and older millennials are dealing with larger debts than previous generations, and wondering whether we are making the right decisions to allow us to be financially prepared for retirement, while also being caught in an increasingly precarious job market between baby boomers who are not retiring and younger millennials and generation Z who are rising quickly. On top of this, we're thinking about how can look after our kids and our ageing parents, while also trying to pay the bills. We have a lot to think about and adapt to, and it seems just as we get used to something, it changes.

How do we pin down an identity that emerges in midlife, given that we have so many options? How do we lock one in and set it for life? How do we say 'This is who I am' in a world that is constantly changing? We can't. And we shouldn't have to. There's a constant, complex interplay between ourselves and the world in which we reside. As a member of generation X, I'm quietly rebelling against landing on a particular identity, staying in one role or locking in one persona, which may have applied to so many (women in particular) in generations before. Because I want to be all the things, but not all things at the same time. Some mornings I'm proudly awake before the birds, but other days I just can't get up after a perimenopause-fuelled sleepless night. I like the idea of dancing the night away, but I also want to stay in. I want to meet someone wonderful, but I also want to stay single. I want to do nothing all day, but I also want to be tremendously successful. I want to be healthy, but I also want to eat a bowl of chips. I want to dress in stylish clothes, but I also just want to wear my black activewear all day. I want my days to be structured and busy, but at the same time pray for a day with nothing in my diary. I want to have long, interesting conversations, but I also don't want to talk. I want to save for the future, but I want to spend on the now. I want to travel the world, but I also want to move to a small remote town in the forest and disconnect from the world around me. Can't there be a grey area? Doesn't being both make us interesting? Isn't the complexity what makes us human? I was more of one before, but now I'm becoming more of the other. But I might go back to the one before later. I don't want to lock in an identity. Doesn't it serve us in a world that's constantly changing that we be more fluid in our approach to identity? Can we not totally make our mind up? I want to fight the impulse to choose one or the other. And a benefit of being a modern-day midlifer is that we can all avoid this choice. We can wonder, ponder, stay open in our minds and watch what experiences life brings in. We don't have to lock anything in.

And let's just hold space for my denim confusion, as I know I'm not alone. My client Serena recently shared her own jeans confusion with me, although her dilemma was entirely different. She said exhaustedly, 'These days are we supposed to buy high-rise jeans and tuck our muffin tops in, or do we buy low-rise jeans and just let them hang over the top?' Fair question, and I'm sure that women in previous generations who fought for the right to wear pants didn't account for this, but in any case, I reckon either option is totally fine.

CHAPTER 4

The Getting of Wisdom

THERE'S A GROUP of young men who rent a house a few doors down from me. With their Beavis and Butt-Head sniggers, they spend every afternoon huddled in their driveway under a makeshift tent staring at their douchebag cars. These guys moved in to my polite, peaceful and leafy street with an egotistical thump a few months ago, replacing a sweet and quiet elderly lady who had lived there for many years. And there they reside still, without a brain cell between them, making far too much noise, mess and probably smell. As you can probably sense, they're not my favourite people in the neighbourhood.

One Saturday afternoon, the kids and I piled into the car and quietly took off down our street. Halfway down the road, I noticed two of the guys standing on the kerb, snickering and pointing like the cavemen they are towards the road. I looked over to see what they were laughing at and noticed the dark blur of a ruckus in the middle of the road – a few birds seemingly having a fight. But as I drove closer, I saw that it was two ravens pecking at a baby magpie lying on its back. I told my kids to look away from this demonstration of the circle of life, but quickly realised the baby magpie was alive and trying to defend itself. At that point I pulled my car over and ran over. I shooed the ravens away, gathered up the little ball of feathery fluff in my hands, looked at the two idiots standing there and in a calm and controlled manner said, 'Are you actual flipping idiots? Just standing there like that. It's a baby bird!' (The 'f' word I used was not 'flipping'.) Then I marched back down the street into my yard cradling the baby, where I checked the bird over and then popped him into a cage to gather his wits. An hour later, my son and I found his little maggie tribe (we already knew them) down the road and the baby flew back to its family. Happy ending.

It's not hard to be an empathic and compassionate human being, to have reverence for life. Yet it was apparently too hard for the bunch of dim-witted young men who (unfortunately) live near me. Once I got back in the car, I turned to my kids who had witnessed the whole episode and said, 'Don't ever be like that when you're older,' imparting some helpful wisdom that will serve them well on their life journey – wisdom about the importance of having empathy for living creatures, which unfortunately the young men had yet to learn.

When I was a kid, we had a shelf full of volumes of the *Encyclopaedia Britannica* in our home to wade through to gain knowledge about the world. I'd flick through the shiny pages, learning about things such as different land formations, the inside of plant cells, rainforests, the journey of Captain Cook and panda habitats. All the knowledge I needed for my daily life was apparently crammed into those 20-plus volumes, which I rigorously studied in the evenings, searching for answers to my school assignments. We are provided with information at school, and we learn to understand and interpret this information which turns into knowledge, but the ability to apply the knowledge comes from our own experiences. This is down to us, and our active participation in life. It's information, plus the understanding of it and applying it. Contrary to what our formal educators tell us, the getting of wisdom mostly comes from life. It comes from immersing ourselves into the richness of life, engaging in the messiness of it all and extracting the gold from it. It takes a lifelong journey of gathering up experiences, learning from them, reflecting on them and growing as a result. Wisdom is gained along the way and applied to our life going forth, so that life can get better for us (and others) in the future.

Us middle-agers know stuff. We know a lot. We have gained a lot of wisdom from our formal education, from other people and from our life experiences. Some of the most important wisdom of all has come from dealing with our own adversities: previous moments of crisis that we found tremendously hard to navigate at the time. Moments that we didn't think we'd get through, perhaps moments that were so fraught with emotion that we couldn't even think straight. Moments that, once the emotions settled, we could start thinking through, start processing, and then start thinking about what we could do make ourselves and our life better. This process becomes the golden life hack for the future: the formula that we will use for similar experiences and the wisdom we will impart onto others. To quote Albert Einstein, 'Wisdom is not a product of schooling, but of the lifelong attempt to acquire it.'

Wisdom helps us notice when we see wrongs in life, and assists us in trying to make them right. Wisdom allows us to empathise with others and build healthy relationships. Wisdom fosters ongoing personal growth and keeps us learning and improving. Wisdom helps us achieve our goals and delay our gratification. Wisdom gives us the strength to go on when life is challenging and feels way too hard. Wisdom helps us understand ourselves better.

And, of course, wisdom helps us to teach our kids not be uncaring in the future, and to always, always save injured baby birds.

CHAPTER 5

The Goal Is Contentment

PHARRELL WILLIAMS SANG a song about it. Philosophers have debated it. Influencers persuade us with their aesthetically perfect Instagram grids to chase it. Advertisers tell us we will be it if we buy their products. And we all seem to aspire to it. Happiness.

When we leave something in our lives, whether it is a place, job or relationship, often we say it's because we don't feel happy. We make endless decisions and choices with the goal of becoming happy. Ultimately, happiness is what we are all aiming for. But what *is* happiness? Is it the same for everyone? Is it all it's cracked up to be? Is it the head honcho of emotions and the rest of them can just grovel at its feet? Or do we need to think about happiness a little more (or, as I'm about to suggest, less) before we establish it as our ultimate goal in life?

While there is no single definition of happiness, it is usually described as a positive emotional state that encompasses feelings of joy, fulfilment and satisfaction. When someone is feeling happy, they're more likely to want to get out of bed in the morning, they will generally have a smile on their face, they usually have a peppy energy about them and often they will show enthusiasm for life. With the advent of easily accessible and on-demand music, I'm not sure if people whistle that much anymore, but if they did, it's likely they'd be whistling because they're happy. Life generally *feels* better when we're happy.

My idea of happiness is different from your idea of happiness. I find happiness in the smallest things, such as long, wandering walks with my dog, moody sunsets, my fiddle leaf fig looking shiny, falling into bed at night (how good is going to bed?) and Reese's Peanut Butter Cups. They all make me feel happy. In fact, sitting here writing this chapter in my home office, in silence, with a nice cup of tea and my cats on the chair next to me makes me happy. But to other people, my little moments of happiness wouldn't cut it (particularly if you're not a cat person).

What makes us happy is subjective. We all have a different happiness currency and, contrary to popular belief, happiness doesn't always come from external pleasures. Some of the happiest people on Earth live in the most impoverished places, demonstrating that happiness may come from something internal. Happiness is not something we have to keep chasing in the outside world but something that resides inside us, like an inner pilot light. It has been there the whole time; we just didn't notice.

American psychologist Martin Seligman believes that humans become happier through pleasure (eating nice food, taking a warm bath); engagement (immersion in a fulfilling activity like training for a marathon, gardening or educational pursuits); relationships (having social ties); meaning (belonging to something bigger than yourself); and accomplishments (achieving tangible goals). As one can imagine, some people find happiness a little bit elusive, and some people are looking for it in all the wrong places. But that's not for us to point out. Some things people need to figure out for themselves, when it's the right time for them.

But happiness isn't the be all and end all of life – if we were supposed to feel happy all the time, we would not have evolved to have the myriad other emotions of the human condition. It would have been a danger to our ancestors to be sitting in endless bliss and joy all day long. We need all the other emotions to keep us on our toes and help us adapt to our environment when life gets tough. All emotions serve important functions in human life, so we shouldn't be putting happiness (and its other 'positive' emotional cronies such as joy, love or satisfaction) on a pedestal as much as we do. We need anger in response to what we perceive as injustices; we need sadness to help us process and cope with loss; we need guilt if we have violated our own values or morals, or even harmed someone else; we need shame so we can self-reflect and self-evaluate when we've done something wrong that could have harmed others. These emotions may help us grow and make better choices in the future. We should aspire to be content with our lives, even though we might feel negative emotions at times.

Contentment is not happiness – it is about being satisfied with our current situation. Feeling a sense of contentment allows us to live in the moment and be at ease with who we are and what we have. If we focus on fostering a sense of contentment in our lives and can savour the good feelings, we can more easily deal with the other emotions that we'll unavoidably feel. Of course, it's nice to have periods of happiness peppered throughout our lives just to 'zhoosh' things up a bit but, as we know, life doesn't always permit that. It is unreasonable and even unrealistic for us to think that we can always be happy. If we live life to its fullest, there are going to be hard times, challenging times and times where it may feel too hard to go on. But the power to keep things in perspective sometimes is enough to pull us out from the depths of despair.

A place of contentment is where we can think clearly, when we are rational; it's when we can make good decisions, solve problems, communicate better with those around us and create what's next for us. Even when we are not satisfied with certain areas of our lives, having a sense of overall contentment connects us with the present moment and soothes our psyche so we can choose the right thing to do next.

But we don't want to do with contentment what we've been trying to do with happiness all our lives, either; we don't want to start chasing it. To quote Elizabeth Gilbert in her book *Eat Pray Love*, 'I have searched frantically for contentment for so many years in so many ways, and all these acquisitions and accomplishments – they run you down in the end. Life, if you keep chasing it so hard, will drive you to death.'

If we stop, sit and listen right now, we can find contentment right here. It's a little hard at first, I know, but throughout this book you will find out how to do it.

PART 2

How to Go From Crisis to Contentment

CHAPTER 6

Develop Emotional Wellbeing

RECENTLY, I BROKE an unwritten rule of mine. A rule that I'd silently created myself, then declared out loud to those who'd listen and applied rigorously to protect myself and my family. It was a serious rule, with dire consequences if broken.

We don't do shopping on a Saturday.

Saturday shopping. I loathe it. I will do anything to avoid the blood, sweat and tears of a suburban shopping centre on a Saturday. I find it a ghastly experience. I'd rather shop online for food, or nonsensically pay twice as much at the local independent grocer or ten times as much to eat out at a (quiet) restaurant. If there was an award for supporting small food businesses in my area, I'd win it. I can rationalise my way out of a Saturday suburban shopping centre visit as quickly as a toddler throwing a tantrum once they've spied a KitKat at the checkout. Speaking of which, shopping centres are usually the shiz to a child (especially when they get what they want). Lollies, toys and babycinos ... everything a small human with no emotional regulation can dream of. Same goes for the egocentric teenager: food, friends, fun and fashion. I get it. I really do. I used to love shopping when I was younger. As a teenager I'd spend all day at the local shopping centre, dopamine hits galore: the latest Levi's over here, ice-cream over there, new shoes over here, cute guy who works in that cafe over there. The local shopping complex was my favourite place to be in my youth. Not anymore. 'Remember guys ... mummy doesn't do shopping on a Saturday,' I've been saying in a Mary Poppins-like voice to my kids for about 16 years, and I've usually been well-organised enough to get away with it.

I can't recall what sparked my slow descent into Saturday shopping hatred. It just crept in over time. Maybe it's the crowds, maybe it's the smells, maybe it's the consumerism, maybe it's the screaming kids, maybe it's the expenditure, maybe it's the noise or maybe I'd just rather be somewhere else. Maybe it's for all those reasons. And then my kids and I recently, in an amnesiac state, proceeded to go shopping on a Saturday.

Of course, as I expected, it was a big mistake. *Big* mistake. And what I can mostly remember from the whole experience was the whingeing and the relentless moaning: 'I'm hungry,' 'I'm thirsty,' 'I'm tired,' 'I'm hot,' 'I'm too cold,' 'I'm not lining up for that,' 'My feet are sore,' 'Ewww, germs,' 'There's too many people. Can we go now?' 'Wahhhhh.' It never stopped. I know what you're thinking. Bloody kids. How irritating. But it wasn't my kids whingeing and moaning. It was me.

It would be remiss of me not to talk about feelings and middle age straight away. In fact, it would be heedless of me as a psychologist not to talk about how feelings affect human beings. They are inextricably connected: feelings cannot be prised away from the human condition. We are feeling creatures who are constantly driven by the emotions that our brain creates in response to what it's perceiving in the world around us. And my brain on a Saturday, at a busy shopping centre, senses way too much; I'm perceiving it as a horrible experience and I'd rather be anywhere else. But first up ... I will complain about it a bit. So, I did.

I've become cognisant of my emotions changing as I get older. I'm by no means an angry person, not even a short-tempered one (I have a helpfully lengthy fuse), but I've observed that I'm pricklier than I used to be, maybe a tad more wary and not as naively peppy. I feel I was much 'nicer' when I was younger, back when I hadn't interacted with the world so much, back in the good old days where I hadn't dealt with the 'slings and arrows of outrageous fortune' (as Hamlet says). I don't really feel that 'nice' anymore. I still *act* nice, mind you, but I've retreated from the world a little bit because I feel irritated by it (and by people in it), so when I do emerge out of my people-free cave I can muster some 'niceness'.

As I get older, so many little things make me feel grumpy. (I know they are all very 'first-world', so let's acknowledge the pettiness straight up – petty but still very much valid, to me at least.) Apart from Saturday shopping, you will also find me grumpy every time I see people who are unfashionably late to concerts holding hot chips and people who drive four-wheel drives who don't go four-wheel driving. Then there are the people who make you wait while they spend an excessive amount of time backing their car into parking spaces when they could have just driven straight into the bay (saving us all the time and grand display of their less-than-impressive reverse-parking skills). Oh, and lining up ... for anything. That annoys me. In the working world: meetings that could have been emails, voice messages longer than one minute and, of course, at the top of the list, mansplainers. At home it's the little things: when my dressing gown's sleeve catches on door handles, when I bite into hard pears, when metal coat hangers get tangled or when the garden hose kinks as soon as I walk to the end of the garden. I especially get annoyed when I can't get my fitted sheet to fit on my bed. There are so many little things to get irritated about ... and so many more big things (don't get me started).

It's well documented that we get grumpier around middle age. A recent Swiss study (2024) found that middle-aged individuals reported lower life satisfaction and joy, as well as higher anger, sadness and worry than younger adults.

Given the number of conversations I have with people about this every day, I feel it's not a matter of *if* we will get grumpy at middle age, but rather *when*. This might manifest as being more agitated, short-tempered, annoyed or even, as one of my clients describes, 'a tad salty'. We can become irritated with what's going on in the world, with our own situation, with our jobs, with the people we are closest to. We tend to be a bit feistier than we once were. One of my clients said to me recently when describing her husband (whom she adores, mind you), 'I just can't even stand looking at his face sometimes.'

These dominating negative emotions can leave middle-aged people in distress, a little too much at times. My client Bianca recently referred to her perimenopause 'journey', which she's been going through for the last three *years*, as an 'emotional shit show' – not one to mince words. Her description would resonate far and wide with the midlife female population who are experiencing the emotional turbulence of this period of life. Dr Louise Newson, a GP and world-renowned expert in menopause, actually adds 'the' at the beginning of this term, as in 'the menopause', declaring it to be a significant time of upheaval. But it's not just women who are navigating emotional upheavals at this time of their lives. Although men tend not to talk about how they are feeling emotionally, they are feeling more than they say they are. Believe me.

Often people ask me what my favourite group of people to work with is, expecting me to say women, or even children. My answer usually is anyone, but I've found working with middle-aged men, grumpy ones in particular, intriguing. Back when I worked in private practice, when I opened my office door to another grumpy, moody middle-aged male, I always knew that we were in for an interesting psychological journey, one that would become quite transformative. In most cases, these men had not booked in to see me off their own back, but rather had been sent by their partner; there was always a reluctant gruffness to their demeanour in their first sessions with me. Depressed, moody, quick to anger, low energy, disappointment with the world and a *massive* intolerance of other people ... this cluster of symptoms is quite common in middle-aged men. Contrary to the stereotype of the younger woman and a sports car, this time of life can often distressingly consist of a non-existent sex life, seemingly no male friends and a penchant for falling asleep in an armchair in front of the telly. None of these things maketh a contented middle-aged man.

There are many moments in life when we feel happiness, joy and love. There are also many moments when we feel annoyed, frustrated or even angry. Feelings are extensions of emotions, and we humans can feel a repertoire of hundreds of emotions. Some can feel sporadic, such as surprise, which disappears as quickly as it arrives. Others, such as fear, can linger a little longer, making us uncomfortably hypervigilant. Some emotions such as love, can envelope us in warmth throughout our body, making us feel safe and secure; while others, such as resentment, can sit stagnant in our body like poison for decades, leaving a permanent scowl and a grudge for all to deal with. We all have emotions, and they are all useful – even the ones usually perceived as negative. What would have become of our ancestors if they didn't feel fear or anger? Would their bodies have known to prepare them to fight predators or run away from them? What would have become of our ancestors if they didn't feel guilt or shame – would they have been kicked out of their tribe, become vulnerable to predators? If they hadn't felt these emotions, would we even be here today to talk about this? Those negative emotions that we tend to become concerned about are often the ones we need to listen to the most, not only for survival – like our ancestors – but to be able to troubleshoot our lives and redirect them if we need to.

Middle age can bring forth a host of negative emotions and, being the emotionally driven creatures we are, it can be easy to become dominated by them. But allowing ourselves to be directed by those negative emotions often means that we stay on a well-trodden path rather than trying to understand what they are telling us, which can lead towards growth. If we sit and listen to these negative emotions, we can gather insight into what's working in our lives and what isn't, making some changes if need be. If we try to understand what they are telling us, we have more information, more data to interpret, which can assist us to make more informed decisions, solve problems, align our actions with our values and goals, all leading towards a more content emotional state. This is the emotional agility we need in midlife. The key is to have the awareness to acknowledge how we are feeling and resist the urge to be driven by our emotions. This allows us to choose the best response: the response that is conscious and well-thought-out and that aligns with our goals and values. It's easy to be irritated now and again in midlife, but it's also very easy to just *become* an irritated person. Instead of reacting irrationally, we need to acknowledge our irritation so we can avoid doing something we might regret later. In fact, research has also shown that people in middle age have a better grasp on handling their emotions and have a tendency to focus on avoiding negativity and seeking out positivity.

As we age, acquiring a regulatory toolkit is necessary so we are resilient and can bounce back to contentment when facing negative experiences.

As American author Glennon Doyle said in her book *Untamed*, 'Feeling all your feelings is hard, but that's what they're for. Feelings are for feeling. All of them. Even the hard ones.' Maybe your anger is telling you you're unhappy at work, maybe the guilt is telling you that you could have handled that differently, maybe the fear is telling you that something's not right and maybe the sadness is teaching you about loss and what you need in your life. These are all powerful emotions that are telling you what might not be working for you, and what actions you might be able to take. Perhaps envy is telling you about something you desire in your life, that you need to ignite your motivation to be successful; resentment is telling you about something that you're holding on to that you need to let go of; irritation is telling you to buy a boxing bag to release some tension; and regret is telling you that you are disappointed about your past decisions or actions – *but* recognising that is a chance to learn and make better decisions in the future.

Us human beings are cursed with negativity bias, so we tend to notice only the negative aspects of our environment. We look around at life and pick apart all the things that are wrong with it (TBH, biting into hard pears is still disappointing; I will never become content about this). Noticing the negative, the threats, the bad would have served our ancestors well – this gave them the information they needed to change, prepare, predict and survive. In the modern world, we want to be able to do all that, but *also* proactively look for the good stuff to elicit a more balanced perspective. We need to learn to let ourselves bathe in positive emotions too, by intentionally noticing and acknowledging what is wonderful, what is good, what is peaceful, and letting those feelings of gratitude linger a little longer than we usually do. It might be a friend who makes us feel happy, a team that gives us a sense of belonging, a neighbour who gives us a taste of kindness, a landscape that allows us to feel awe, a book that elicits wonder, some alone time to give us serenity, our children who make us feel playful, or the arms of a partner who makes us feel loved.

It's not just denying the hard stuff, nor emphasising the good stuff, that brings us contentment at middle age. It's the acceptance of all these emotions, positive and negative. To quote from the Serenity Prayer, 'Grant me the serenity to accept the things I cannot change, the courage to the change the things I can, and the wisdom to know the difference.'

And my wisdom is to not go shopping on a Saturday.

Considerations

Have you been experiencing any negative emotions recently?

What specific challenges have you identified?

What are your strengths in this area?

What specific actions can you take to move towards feeling more content?

Challenge

Mindful Journaling

Mindful journaling is a great way to reflect on how you've been feeling and why. Choose a comfortable, quiet place where you can write without interruptions. Allocate 10–15 minutes for your journaling session to ensure you have ample time to explore your emotions. Begin by writing about your current emotional state. You might use prompts such as 'What emotions am I feeling right now?' or 'What triggered these emotions?' Write in a way that focuses on observing your emotions without judging or criticising yourself. Aim to describe your feelings and their physical sensations. Reflect on what might have triggered your emotions and how you've responded. Consider any patterns or recurring themes. End your session by noting a few things you're grateful for or positive aspects of your day, as this can shift your focus towards more positive emotions in the short-term and the long-term. Occasionally review your past entries to identify patterns or insights into your emotional responses, and what might be helpful to soothe you in the future.

Commitment

Going forward
I commit to these
new rituals to help
process, understand
and manage my
emotions better
over time ...

CHAPTER 7

Shift Thoughts

WHEN I WAS in primary school, I found it difficult to get to sleep. I'd lie wide-eyed in the darkness, thoughts constantly streaming like ticker tape through my mind, sometimes pondering things about the world such as, 'What's outside the universe?', 'Where do old seagulls go to die?' and 'Why did the Santa Claus at the school Christmas pageant have hands just like my dad?' But like many of us lying awake in our beds at night, the thoughts that dominated were mostly negative. I'd be worrying about something random but extremely scary and getting myself into quite the internal tizz: 'What if my parents die?' 'What will happen if the sun burns out while I'm asleep?' Or the most serious moral dilemma of them all, 'What would I actually wish for if I had three wishes?' This noisy inner dialogue always seemed to happen in the quiet darkness, pushing sleep out even further, rendering me more anxious and awake.

It's not just kids who experience a wild inner dialogue. Many of us go through much of our lives with a 'monkey mind' that is restless and easily distracted, thoughts crisscrossing in different directions. I've managed to tame the wild animal in my head with the skills I've learned as a psychologist, so I don't tend to sit in the distress of negative thoughts for too long these days, but my mind still chats away regardless. Like, *all the time*. I can have quite the internal conversation with just me, myself and I. Sometimes I have deeply intellectual conversations with myself that lead me to hours-long research journeys ('Hmm, I wonder if middle managers are more susceptible to burnout than any other level in an organisation?'). My thoughts can sometimes be health related and give me a jolt of anxiety ('That mole's looking weird; better get that checked'); they can be global ('Why are governments spending billions to explore outer space when we have fish in the deep ocean trenches with little lights on their heads?'); they can be practical ('Do I have enough quinoa in the cupboard to make that salad for dinner?'); they can be ruminations on regret ('Did I say something obtuse to that hot tradie at my house yesterday?'); and they also can be downright random ('Whatever happened to Huey Lewis and the News?'). All of this can go through my mind in mere minutes.

Apart from my newly emerged middle-aged popcorn brain, I'm noticing that my mind is a tad foggy at times. Attempting to retrieve one thought out of an intertwined knot of them in my mind is like trying to pick out a stuffed toy from a claw machine – mostly impossible. If I manage to blow away the fog a tad and think for a moment, I could conclude that midlife is mucking my mind about. One minute I can be an intellectual whippet, full of knowledge, opinions and quick wit. But within seconds I can become a complete airhead, with not a whit of intellect to impart on anyone. I can oscillate between the two extremes within mere minutes. My teenagers have pointed out on numerous occasions that I have moments of cutting myself off when I'm talking and staring off into the distance for no apparent reason. They've aptly named this the 'wondering Mum' look. If it's not the brain fog clogging up my thinking intermittently, I also seem to be more forgetful. Even mid-sentence, word salad can just take over what was once a perfectly articulate and coherent thought. It's been on my mind recently to order a Jim Kwik book to help with my midlife (likely perimenopausal) memory issues, but I keep forgetting to order it.

Let's face it: there's a lot going on the minds of us middle-aged adults. What were once tasks shared by a whole village are now expected to be done by just one person in our modern society. We're always working, planning, stressing, anticipating, preparing and organising, not just for ourselves but sometimes on behalf of everybody else, too. And it seems that we spend a lot of time with people who can't think for themselves (I'm looking at you, partners, kids, teenagers, new employees, elderly parents …). In any case, a midlifer's mental load is rather heavy, and you will hear our excessive cries of 'I'm busy' spoken far and wide (but mostly texted).

Most of my work with people involves presenting at workplace events, and at every seminar or workshop I run, I ask the crowd how they are feeling (because, being a psychologist, I can't help myself). Without fail, 'overwhelmed' is yelled out. More than any other word. This is in every workplace setting I visit. 'Overwhelm' typically refers to a feeling of being inundated or overcome, often by a large volume of tasks, responsibilities, duties, emotions or challenges (personally and professionally). When someone is overwhelmed, they may feel unable to cope or manage effectively due to the sheer magnitude or intensity of what they're facing, which is more than their psychological capabilities can handle. This can manifest as feelings of stress, anxiety or helplessness (or all three). And when we hold onto this for a long period of time and don't shift these emotions, we can become burnt out.

Burnout isn't always caused by the occupational stress that arises because of unhealthy workplace systems. Often it's the sheer amount of thinking that's involved in getting through the day. One of my clients, Alyssa, a teacher with three children of her own, said that her mind is always filled to the brim. She's constantly making sure that everyone is alright, that everything is organised for everyone in the family and that everyone is where they need to be. Her mother-duck mind won't settle until she knows everything is in place and everyone in her family is okay. She doesn't have even an amoeba-sized space for any more thought.

In fact, she claims that she doesn't even know what else she thinks about. Like Alyssa, many middle-agers are busy working, and much of our brain space during the day is consumed with thoughts about our jobs. But layered over that of course are the multiple other roles we have. It wasn't that long ago (and is still the case in some cultures) that most people had a more limited role, but now the 'do it all', 'you can have everything you want' culture is wearing us thin. We're having trouble thinking straight.

But within the sheer overwhelm of midlife duties and responsibilities, different ways of thinking that were never there before can emerge. Middle-agers often start reconsidering their place in the world, and their inner dialogue begins brewing new thoughts. Of course, people's specific thoughts can vary widely based on individual circumstances, values and priorities, but many find themselves spending a lot of time contemplating various aspects of their life at middle age. If I were to undertake a thematic analysis of conversations I have engaged in with my midlife clients over the years, the most common topics would be their extended family's dynamics; parental duties; relationships with partners (and exes); ageing parents and friends (or lack thereof); financial concerns; work (with the main highlights being unreasonable workloads, irritating colleagues, unhealthy systems and, of course, management); increasing concerns about physical health; and personal and professional issues that are impacting their mental wellness.

But among the weave of conversations about the tapestry of what is important in their life emerges some existential thinking about their life purpose, their legacy and their impact on the world. From my experience, among the mixed feelings, chaos and discontent that sometimes arise during the busyness of middle age, people start thinking a little differently about life.

At times, particularly if we have a host of negative experiences under our belts, midlife can make us feel anxious and wary about the world. In an attempt to protect us, our brains can whip out the cognitive distortions like rapid fire. Cognitive distortions are irrational patterns of thinking that many of us partake in, which negatively affect our perceptions and, in turn, our emotions. Cognitive distortions can cause us to jump to conclusions (without all the necessary information), catastrophise (assuming the worst-case scenario), partake in black-and-white thinking (without entertaining the grey area) or personalise (incorrectly believing everything is related to us). We might even be one for a bit of fortune-telling now and again, making negative predictions about future events based on our past experiences, without evidence. If we get stuck in a distorted way of thinking this can cause a crisis. Some middle-aged people can stagnate in their own ways, stuck in old unhelpful beliefs and intellectual inertia, ceasing to grow at all. Human beings are thinking creatures. We think, we plan and we worry. We can have thousands of thoughts a day going through our heads. This is what makes us such powerful creatures: we can be consciously present in the moment, but we can also refer (consciously and unconsciously) back to the past, and then use that information to predict and prepare for the future. Although this is enormously useful, it comes at a cost. All of us have automatic thinking styles, and some of them are not particularly helpful. Neglecting to question the way we think could not only be doing us a disservice but causing us necessary distress. Maybe if we had a different thinking style, we could be happier, more confident or more successful. Some of our thoughts are intentional, such as when we deliberately try to remember what ingredients we need to cook a meal, or what we need to do at work today. Other thoughts are automatic, such as we when judge other people or ourselves too quickly or when we entertain what-ifs and worries that aren't necessarily reasonable. This is where the trouble lies.

In therapy, people often work on changing the way they feel by questioning and challenging their thoughts to overcome any biases in them. Just because we think it, doesn't mean it's right. The idea is that if we think about our thinking a bit more, we can come up with a better alternative. We might catastrophise and blow things out of proportion, viewing every problem as near the end of the world. Maybe we magnify other people's positive attributes and minimise our own. Maybe our thoughts are too black and white.

Maybe we personalise too much and blame ourselves for everything that goes wrong when it probably has nothing to do with us. Thoughts are not facts. If we midlifers begin observing our thoughts, pulling ourselves away from our cognitive distortions and learning to interpret our thoughts in a healthier way, we can get better at problem-solving, challenging ourselves and creating new ideas to improve our lives in the present moment and in the future.

Among the hustle and bustle of adulthood is the growing of wisdom. Using this newfound wisdom, we often start questioning more, challenging conventions and seeking out different perspectives – sometimes even breaking free of old unhelpful beliefs. In many cases, we get smarter and become more curious, and through the integration of all of this new thinking comes a different world view. This is gold that we can apply to our life. Yes, we might be applying it to questions such as, 'What am I going to have for dinner?' (which is, quite frankly, extremely important). But we might also ask, 'What do I want to do with my life? What do I want to change? Where do I want to go? What's it all about? Should I be doing something different?' Thinking differently makes life a little different. Instead of sleepwalking through life, we're steering it with a conscious mind.

American psychoanalyst Erik Erikson developed a theory of eight stages of psychosocial development, and his concept of 'generativity versus stagnation' is the stage that lands in middle age. Erikson proposed that individuals navigating this stage start looking outwards a little more, taking note of their place in and impact on the world, and start thinking a little differently about their contributions to society and future generations. They look outwards from their homes, up from their own work, and think about what else they can do to help with the global condition. This would explain that I see people in midlife volunteering at animal shelters, writing books about their own life adversities to inspire others or starting to think about what they can do to help their older children get a head start in life. The worries begin turning into action.

Despite the stereotype of middle-agers becoming more set in our ways, many people in midlife maintain a strong desire for learning more. I see many pursue new interests, hobbies or educational opportunities, expanding their knowledge about the world and staying intellectually engaged. In the last couple of years, I've never seen so many midlife people keen to challenge their minds, whether it be by reading personal development books, enrolling in new professional courses, learning new languages or taking up a new creative endeavour. I've got middle-aged clients who are learning Italian, clients volunteering in industries they've never worked in and clients creating 'nature rooms' in their workplaces so they can meditate at lunchtime. As they start clawing back time for their own purposes, they start bringing in new information, new thoughts, new ideas, and start diluting what was once dominating their world view, giving them more clarity about what they want to spend time doing in the future.

The more I know, the more I realise I don't know, and the more I want to learn. Sometimes I get myself into a tizz thinking that I don't have enough time to learn the depths of what I really desire to learn more about. I've always had a deep fascination with Egypt and although I've read a few books and watched every documentary I can get my hands on, I still want to learn more.

Oh, and those little deep-sea fish with the lights on their heads? Pffff, who wants to find aliens when we have those little guys swimming out in our oceans?

Considerations

Have you been experiencing any uncomfortable or unhelpful thoughts recently?

What specific challenges have you identified?

What are your strengths in this area?

What specific actions can you take to move towards feeling more content?

Challenge

Thought Record Exercise

Thinking about your thinking can create a healthier thinking style. To detect your unhelpful thinking habits (cognitive distortions), start by identifying a distressing thought you have recently experienced – such as 'I always mess up at work' or 'Everyone is annoyed at me' – and write it down. Next, categorise the distortion (e.g. jumping to conclusions, catastrophising, black-and-white thinking, personalisation or fortune-telling) and assess the evidence for and against this thought by noting specific examples. Then, create more balanced and realistic alternative thoughts based on this evidence, such as 'I've made mistakes but also have many successes. I can improve' or 'Yes, my kids might be a little annoyed right now, but most people enjoy my company.' Reflect on how the original thought affects your emotions compared to the alternative thought. Practise this regularly to become more aware of and adjust your unhelpful thinking, leading to a healthier thinking style.

Commitment

Going forward
I commit to
these new rituals
to help me shift
to more helpful
thinking styles ...

CHAPTER 8

Boost Wellness & Vitality

MANY YEARS AGO, when I was a teenage psychology undergraduate, I had a discussion with one of my male university lecturers. He had recently returned to lecturing after taking a lengthy leave of absence to deal with a heart issue and subsequent cardiovascular disease diagnosis. As I was standing in his office, focused on seeking some assistance with my research assignment, he casually muttered about the downsides of ageing and how quickly illness can creep up on you. 'Everything starts falling apart after 40, Marny,' he warned as he squinted at my paper on his desk. I was more concerned at the time about my assignment than his scaremongering about what could happen when I was super old, but his warning had an impact, subconsciously at least. His words have stuck with me.

Even for those of us lucky enough not to have been cursed with too many health concerns in our earlier years, inevitably some issues with our bodies do start to creep in as we journey through middle age. As an active and healthy middle-aged woman now, I often reflect on whether my lecturer was onto something. One of the first things I have noticed is that I seem to be in pain more. I'm either in pain because I'm injured, because I'm healing from an injury, because I haven't exercised a body part properly or because I've exercised *too* much. Some of the most severe pain, of course, has come from injuries I acquired from doing ... basically nothing. Like opening the fridge to pull out the mayonnaise, opening a drawer to grab some socks, or just sneezing. Many of my middle-aged clients feel a similar way, hobbling into our sessions, yearning to tell me dramatic tales of the wild *Survivor*-type adventures that caused their ankle to fracture, their shoulder to freeze or their knee to buckle. But, alas, it's usually a stock-standard story that falls under the category of 'just getting older'. Although ageing is a slow, gradual process, it feels as though it's snuck up on us by the time we hit middle adulthood, as things start changing a bit more rapidly than they did when we were younger. One minute we're busting moves to 'Tainted Love' on the dance floor until 5am, and the next we're tucked up in bed by 9pm, stinking of Tiger Balm with a massage pillow behind our necks. Everything seems to feel a little different – a little sorer, a little softer and a little saggier – and it has happened far, far too quickly.

Random body parts that aren't technically injured are in pain, too, for no apparent reason. As a large-breasted woman, I am in pain most days just from carrying my breasts around on my body. They've always been there, and I don't remember being in pain when I was younger. But now they hurt my back, neck and shoulders. I have had moments where I just want a break from having them on me. Should I get a reduction? Perhaps I need to invent a bra that has a special halter attached to something other than my own shoulders. Perhaps I need some trapezius implants. Perhaps I could hire someone to stand behind me and hold them up to take the weight off my back for half an hour a day, a bit like Janet Jackson on the September 1993 *Rolling Stone* magazine cover. She must have felt such relief.

Being a health psychologist with an interest in pain, I have explored time and time again with my adult clients the interesting phenomenon that is the psychology of chronic pain. Many of them have long-term pain from a previous injury that their doctors have shown has physically healed, yet their brain still produces pain – real pain. The likely explanation from neuroscientists is that the chronic pain experienced by many patients who have no current *physical* injury is likely to be caused by unresolved *emotional* pain from long ago.

The area of the brain that predominantly processes physical pain is called the anterior cingulate cortex, and right next to it is the area where we feel emotional pain. If we don't process our emotions as they need to be processed, the brain will turn on a physical pain signal instead. This is why pain management plans often involve the patient working with a psychologist to help them understand and manage their emotional responses and modify unhelpful thoughts, which can be exacerbating their pain. By the time we get to middle age, we have often dealt with our fair share of emotional pain. Some of us have processed our emotions along the way and are still feeling quite spritely, while others are constantly cracking and creaking our way through life with lingering pain from undealt-with or even repressed emotional pain from a long time ago. I'm lucky to have the expertise to be able to take the lesser pain route: if I'm going to be in pain, it's going to be on my terms. My pain tends to be greater if I don't exercise, which means the pains I'm talking about are lesser than the pains I would get if I wasn't exercising so much. Better to be in pain and able to bounce back if injured than being in pain with no resilience at all.

At its worst, middle age can bring unexpected health conditions; at its best, it can bring natural physical changes that *feel* like nasty health conditions – such as menopause. One of the most common conversations I have about health crises with my midlife female clients is about menopause and its not-so-friendly pre-emptive neighbour, perimenopause. For some women, this stage of life can pass them by like a subtle breeze, but for others, it can hit them like a cyclone. Middle age typically marks the onset of perimenopause for women, with its various physical health changes that can cause years of unpleasant symptoms. It's described as part of the natural ageing process for women (and hence has historically been glossed over in health discussions) but its impact on women's wellbeing has been underestimated. The combination of uninvited changes in hormones, reproductive health, bone density, skin elasticity, body composition, cardiovascular health and mental health can impact women for years. One of the more welcome changes is the slow cessation of menstrual periods, but even they, for the most part, don't go out without a bit of drama. And just when you think they've gone, they will sometimes come back for one last (unexpected) hurrah, which is exactly what happened to my poor client, whom we shall call 'Carrie' after the Stephen King character that popped into my mind when she was telling me a descriptive story of an unfortunate 'accident' at the post office.

As if perimenopause wasn't anxiety-inducing enough, another client of mine morphed from a healthy, energetic woman into a rather unwell, lethargic bag of nerves with a cluster of odd symptoms in the space of a week. Her symptoms included heart palpitations, severe fatigue, body aches, tingling fingers, neck rash, frequent urination and nauseating anxiety. Like way too many of us, she turned to the internet, which unhelpfully diagnosed her with about ten different diseases including type 2 diabetes, cardiovascular disease, lupus, cancer, an overactive thyroid (and an underactive thyroid) and multiple sclerosis, all of which made her panic even more. Funnily enough, Dr Google didn't diagnose her with perimenopause, which her

GP helpfully did once she'd built up the courage to see her.

Middle-aged men don't get off lightly in the physical health change department, either. Although they probably would agree that women get it a tad tougher (and if they don't … they should look out) they are still suffering, too. In private practice, I've talked to many middle-aged men over the years who are concerned because they've been drinking way too much; a bit embarrassed that they have woken up with a 'dad bod' they can't seem to shift; riddled with confusion and embarrassment (even sheer panic) about unexpected difficulties with sexual function; and concerned as to why they just can't sleep anymore.

Middle age is commonly associated with the onset of many age-related health issues: we may be diagnosed, some of us for the first time, with a chronic illness such as arthritis, type 2 diabetes or hypertension, or at least begin to endure a series of minor health inconveniences such as acid reflux, tooth abscesses and bunions. These are little nudges that our brain and body start giving us to communicate that the natural progression of ageing is underway, whether we like it or not.

'It's only going to get worse if I don't do anything about it.' This was a life-changing statement one of my clients, Michael, said in a session one day. Not only had it followed an 'aha moment' from our lengthy conversation about the importance of looking after our bodies, but it was the beginning of one of the biggest physical and psychological transformations I had ever witnessed as a psychologist. After decades of back pain, this busy, reasonably healthy but overweight and exhausted middle-aged man had finally had enough. I'd been seeing him for over a year to address his burnout symptoms and coping strategies for managing work-related stress. His sessions with me focused on identifying his maladaptive thought patterns and improving his self-care practices, through which a new physical activity regimen emerged. He ended up starting his days with a personal trainer, and within six months was fitter than he had been as a teenager.

As we reach middle age, we become more cognisant of our mortality and in addition, potential morbidity. This awareness often prompts us to reassess our lifestyle choices and prioritise our health and wellbeing to maintain quality of life as we age. Obviously, there are many people who take their physical health seriously from a very early age with the goal of enjoying a longer, more fulfilling life. But many don't. Many are stiff or in pain, many feel like they are running on empty, many are fatigued, some are constantly sick and rundown, and many just don't physically feel like they used to. In other cases, good health is not a choice, as for many people it's not something that's in their control, and their health conditions are something they have to learn to manage to their best of their ability with the resources they have access to. The Australian Commission on Safety and Quality in Health Care estimates that 60 per cent of

Australians have low health literacy, so it's likely that many people will get to a crisis point with their health as they get older.

Middle age is also a time of reflection, where we may look back on our past health choices and the impact these have had on our health and wellbeing, wondering how different our bodies, our health or even our fitness levels would be if we had chosen a different path long ago; what if we hadn't smoked for so long, what if we had a better diet and what if we were more physically active?

We may be disappointed by our own inertia, but recognising the consequences of unhealthy habits or neglecting self-care in earlier years can inspire middle-agers to make positive health changes. We might start noticing the effects of these choices not only in ourselves, but in people around us. There's nothing as sobering as watching the result of decades of unhealthy lifestyle choices in one of your own ageing parents; it's almost like watching your future self at the end of one fork in the road.

There is something about moving into middle age and all the changes that this time bestows on us, uncomfortable or otherwise, that can awaken us and steer us onto a healthier path. We've just got to take notice of it. It might be the puffing when we're chasing after the kids in the backyard. It might be no longer having the energy for hiking with our mates. It might be the 'sleep divorce' requested by our partner. It might be the back pain that renders us incapacitated every few weeks. It might be the stack of pillows we have to sleep propped up against to ease our heartburn. It might be the sexual difficulties. It might be the grinding in our knees every time we get up from the couch. Experiencing these changes firsthand can serve as a reality check, an awakening for us midlifers to start taking much-needed measures to maintain our health and vitality. Those people who have been proactive in maintaining healthy lifestyle behaviours and heed their doctor's advice often have longer and healthier lives. But it's never too late to start. Ageing its more modifiable than we might think.

I've seen middle-aged men taking up dance classes, middle-aged women learning to run marathons, men in their early 30s quitting drinking, women in their 40s taking up basketball, men in their 50s starting Pilates, women in their 50s starting CrossFit and couples in their mid-50s training for triathlons, transforming and reinventing themselves into a healthier state than they had ever thought possible.

One of the most common conversations I have with my midlife clients is around sleep, or lack thereof. It comes up in pretty much every conversation I have. There's nothing better than getting a peaceful night's sleep, but for many middle-agers, a whole night's sleep is something we can only dream of (if only we could get some sleep). Sleeping is crucial for good health, and in this multiple-role, many-hat-wearing stage of life, we are in danger of forgetting this. We need sleep to conserve energy, recover from our day's activities, consolidate memory, restore bodily functions, keep our immune system in check and get us back to some sort of balanced state after a productive day. We need sleep to function optimally. But since the invention of the light bulb, us humans have been sleeping less and less, to our own detriment. We're advanced enough to have invented the smart phone, but our brains and bodies haven't evolved enough to cope with the effects of the massive sleep debt often caused by them.

Sleep disorders are a large and under-recognised problem in many developed countries, contributing to a plethora of physical and psychological health conditions. Sleeplessness is a more common complaint from middle age. Maintaining a routine of restful slumber is a key factor in helping to stave off feeling one's true age. According to a recent study by psychologists in Sweden, just two nights of broken sleep are enough to make people feel years older than they are. On average, people in the study felt more than four years older when they were restricted to only four hours of sleep for two consecutive nights, with some even claiming the sleepiness made them feel decades older. Being a perimenopausal woman, I was getting by on about three hours of sleep per night a few months ago, so by this calculation it's no wonder I was feeling 243 years old.

Sleep is something many people think little about until a problem arises. About one in three people suffer from sleep issues at some stage in their life, with many people experiencing chronic sleep problems that span years. Our modern sleeping behaviours are pushing our bodies past what they have evolved to do, and we're subsequently feeling the consequences. In many cases, it's a simple tweak of our habits that's needed. Us humans are wired to be awake in the daylight and asleep when it is dark. We should be going to bed at night and getting up in the morning at roughly the same time every day. We should be giving our bodies a reason to be tired at night because we are moving them during the day. We shouldn't be staring at backlit blue-light devices that mimic sunlight late in the evening. Caffeine in the evening? Forget about sleeping. Excessively long naps in the day and then trying to sleep that night? You just built up a sleep surplus, so why would you be tired? Sleeping will give us our health back, and having good health will give us more life.

The aches and pains of middle age are the information we need to make a difference to our health. Our bodies are usually giving us signs as to what we need, we've just got to stop and listen. Tap into that wisdom. Investing in our health will maximise our longevity and give us the quality of life we want in later years.

Considerations

Are you experiencing any issues in relation to your physical health?

What specific challenges have you identified?

What are your strengths in this area?

What specific actions can you take to move towards feeling more content?

Challenge

Comprehensive Physical Exam

Getting a health check can give help put you on a pathway to wellness and vitality. Book an appointment to see your general practitioner in the coming weeks. A check-up with your doctor will assess your overall health, identify any potential issues, and provide personalised recommendations about the positive steps you can take in the right direction to boost wellness and vitality. Once you've had this appointment and have identified which areas of your physical health need a little more attention, you can start setting some goals to get you on a pathway to better health. This might involve exercising more, eating a more nutritious diet, taking medication, seeing a healthcare specialist or taking steps to move away from some unhealthy practices that could be impacting your health. Talking to your doctor and assessing your overall physical health in its current state gives you the valuable information you need to head in a healthy direction.

Commitment

Going forward
I commit to these
new rituals to help
me become more
aware of the status
of my physical
health, and what
I need to action to
boost wellness ...

CHAPTER 9

Build Love & Connection

PSYCHOLOGY SAYS THAT we chase what's familiar to us. So, do you look like your dog, too? I have a five-year-old husky cross, Chilly. She's tall and long legged, with long black eyelashes and vanilla-coloured hair. If she were human – and I believe she is very close to that – she'd be tall and long legged, with long black eyelashes and blonde hair ... Okay, okay, she'd be me. This dog of mine, whom I adore and, truth be told, spend more time with than any other living creature, humans included, is a very interesting character. She is intelligent and very particular about what she likes and dislikes. If she doesn't know you, she'll sit silently, watching to suss you out before she connects with you. She might take a while to warm up to you and is quite choosy about who she befriends. Once she chooses you and there's mutual, trusting connection, she will be loyal until the end of time. But if you're the type of person to move too quickly, or you do her wrong, she'll snap. After her long walks she sits in her own cushioned rocking chair and looks out of the window, unnecessarily judging everyone who walks by.

One would think that Chilly is a rescue, given her over-analysis of every interaction. She is not a rescue and has been lathered with unconditional love since she was a pup. Perhaps earlier on, in the 12 whole weeks before she lived with me, someone hurt her, and she's held on to it ever since. Who knows. Apart from her judging behaviours, I have recently come to the conclusion that Chilly is a reflection of my inner self – my soul dog. We both like walks, we enjoy food, we're protective of those we love, we can tell by your energy if you're not a good person, we're fiercely loyal, we don't like being manipulated and we might bite if you try to hurt us.

By the time we head into midlife, many of us adults have had a few romantic relationships. We've lusted, loved, longed and laughed. Some of these relationships or past intimate encounters might be peppered with difficult moments that we'd rather forget, some might make us smile and some we might benignly stalk on Facebook to see what they're up to. And of course, some just make us cringe a little and we swiftly change the subject when our friends bring them up over a glass of wine. Sometimes the all-consuming feelings of love we had in the past were unrequited. The mental dress rehearsal never quite made it to opening night, and the person we longed for is now living the life we thought we'd have ... with someone else (and of course, their partner is ghastly and a terrible person on top of that). Other times our relationship memories are shared with the person who is sitting right beside us on the couch watching *Dancing with the Stars*. In any case, every relationship, every love and every moment of connection has shaped who we are today, for better or for worse.

It's like after we finished high school, we all roughly came out of the gates at the same age, but the years have steered us all in different relationship directions. Some found love quickly, some settled down, some travelled solo for years and some spent a lot of time sowing their proverbial oats throughout early adulthood. Over time, people change, life changes and relationship statuses change. Even those who found love early while others were still sniffing around might start to slow down a bit, while others fire up serious relationships later, and some go right off their original track. By midlife we are all running very different races.

When we get to midlife, some people are separated, divorced or even widowed. Some still haven't found the right person. And some people are in relationship limbo, almost like relationship 'presenteeism' – physically there, but psychologically elsewhere. 'I just don't know what I'm going to do,' says Cameron, my mid-50s client who has been married for 20-plus years. 'I guess we're just going through the motions. We've got the boys to think of. It's all just too hard.' For those who've heavily invested in long-term partnership and family, choosing what to do when things are not working is incredibly difficult. Sometimes so much so that no decision is made and the relationship remains stagnant for years. I see this time and time again: middle-aged couples living in discontent for far too long, neither dipping their toes back into the relationship to see if it will work nor leaving it. The reasons for this are many and varied, but the conscious thoughts preventing people from separating usually revolve around their kids, their families, the cost of living, their religion or even just the energy it will take. Something unspoken, though, is that it can be about fear: fear of loneliness, fear of change, fear of judgement, fear of rejection and fear of being out of their (un)comfort zone. But without steps taken either way, the inevitable emotions creep in: frustration, anger, resentment ... even contempt.

While the overall divorce rate in Australia has declined, there's an upward trend in separation among baby boomers and older generation Xers. The Australian Bureau of Statistics' recent findings indicate that the highest divorce rate is among those aged 40–49. These figures suggest that a psychological rumbling is happening at this time of life (for our generation in particular), and it's propelling us out of relationships.

Societal changes have removed the stigma once associated with divorce. Research shows that attitudes have shifted towards being more supportive of divorce in the last three decades. People are more comfortable with navigating these life changes without feeling the social shame that our own parents and grandparents would have faced decades before. Divorce is a positive option for those who feel that they have grown apart and want to move on with their lives separately. It gives our generation the choice to step away from our love lives if we don't feel content in them. Divorce has also been such an important tool for women to untangle their lives (and their children's lives) from abusive men.

Reasons are diverse for separating are diverse. I've seen people longing for a deeper connection with someone, not just to coexist. Perhaps once the kids leave home couples who've parked some of their own issues while focusing on their kids are finally confronted with the elephant in the room, but they have been so distant from each other for so long that it's almost too uncomfortable to step back in. It's hard to be 'in' a relationship when you've been 'out' of it for so long, albeit under the same roof. Life stresses can play a part in the downfall of a relationship: issues with parenting, work and family life can diminish the personal intimacy that is required to keep a relationship alight. Unresolved feelings and emotions such as anger, frustration and resentment – strong emotions that aren't communicated but rather held onto – can lead to disconnect, reduce feelings of empathy and diminish sexual intimacy, all of which required to build trust, love and respect in a relationship. All too often I see people moving further and further apart so that their concerns about their own sexual needs remain unnoticed, to the point that they become so emotionally disconnected that the personal intimacy is non-existent, rendering sex too uncomfortable to talk about.

The midlife struggle to attend to our own needs while remaining connected to our partner and supporting their needs often plays out in intimate settings. When one partner is repeatedly tending to the needs of the other for the stability of the relationship, it takes a toll, both physically and emotionally. Pleasing our partner at the expense of ourselves can compromise our own integrity and cause discontent. I have worked with many middle-aged people who are longing for freedom, to have time to themselves, to realign themselves with life, to not please anyone but themselves, and after separating, they are in no rush whatsoever to move into another relationship.

Whatever our relationship status, midlife is a time of reflection. Some feel that their relationship is solid, and they are looking forward to growing old with their partner, while others are feeling anything but solid, as though they have lost their footing and don't know which way to step next. This can cause considerable discontent as they ponder their feelings and think about what's working, what isn't, whether the relationship is worth fighting for, whether it's better for everyone if they just walk away or, for those who haven't found a partner and deeply want to, whether they need to put a little more effort into finding someone. The crisis happens when things aren't sitting right with us.

People will often turn to mental health professionals to assist them in making the right choices about their relationship, or lack thereof. Some people work hard to rekindle what they once had. If people didn't want to try to make their relationships work, marriage counsellors wouldn't be in business and us psychologists would certainly have less to do. Other times a therapist might help with something more specific: conscious separating, navigating divorce or, a common topic I've discussed with midlifers, how to find your dating prowess again when you haven't dated for 20-plus years.

After they've got help, I've seen many middle-aged people part ways, but I've also seen the reinvigoration of relationships and people really getting to know each other again once their children have left the nest. After separation, some have found the love of their life, others have found a companion and others have decided to keep things open. 'I don't want to be locked into one person. I've been married for over 30 years, and I just want to be free to spend time with different types of people,' my client Joe told me.

Along with all the other changes in midlife, relationships also change, and with two people in a relationship changing at roughly the same time, there is bound to be upheaval. But evaluating ourselves and what we need, along with reflecting on the relationship we are in and having a little more time on our hands to listen to the answers, can lead to a more fulfilling direction for everyone involved. There's no one-size-fits-all approach to love and relationships, but digging deep into who we are and what we need will give us answers.

Considerations

Are you experiencing any concerns in relation to your relationship(s)?

What specific challenges have you identified?

What are your strengths in this area?

What specific actions can you take to move towards feeling more content?

Challenge

Relationship Timeline

To help you understand your relationship's evolution it can be helpful to allocate some time to look back on your relationship. Find a comfortable space where you can work without any distractions. Use a large sheet of paper or pages in a journal. Draw a long horizontal line across the centre of the paper. This will represent the timeline of your relationship. Label the start of the timeline with the date you first met or began your relationship. Proceed horizontally across the line noting the dates on the top, and the corresponding key events or milestones in your relationship under the line. These may include your first date, important anniversaries, major life events (e.g. moving in together, travelling, first baby etc.), achievements and challenges. Look for patterns such as times of growth, recurring challenges or major changes. Take a moment to reflect on the impact each event had on your relationship, celebrate the milestones, think about recurring issues or patterns that may need attention and set some future goals for your relationship moving forward.

Commitment

Going forward
I commit to these
new rituals to help
highlight and work
on areas of my
relationship that
may need attention
and action ...

CHAPTER 10

Nurture Family

'IT'S LITERALLY ASH.'

This is what my 15-year-old son said to me as we both stared at the oven tray where what was once capsicum had been roasting, but which now looked like a school project depicting Pompeii. 'I'm sure we can salvage something,' I muttered, searching for some shiny red sections to tear away from each piece of charcoal to place into our as yet unmade salad.

A burned dinner is not uncommon in my household. Now, I enjoy cooking and I'm adept at it – in fact, I would go so far as to say I am a 'good cook' – which really says something, doesn't it? I possess a large collection of cookbooks, an enormous selection of recipes saved on my Instagram account and my own 'special' dishes that I bring to people's houses, and I would prefer eating my own creations for dinner over ordering in. But if I must cook a wholesome dinner on top of dropping off and picking up one child from basketball training, dropping off and picking up the other from jujitsu, walking the dog, taking a phone call, finishing off my own work for the day and getting to the grocer's, there are risks involved. Ash, literally, may be served up for dinner.

Middle age is full on. It's often the busiest time of our lives. We have a lot on our plates and, for many people, kids can take up much of said plate. If we plonked a pie on that plate (to mix metaphors), we'd probably find that our children would eat up most of it. But over time, adults slowly start getting a few slivers of that pie back as their children grow up, become more independent and integrate into society on their own. I don't think that parents ever get the full pie again, but over the course of a couple of decades of child rearing, you do get more pieces for yourself. Parenting is a journey that changes constantly over the decades of our lives.

I find it interesting to drive past local parks on the weekend, observing young families spending quality time together in the outdoors. I see tired young mums holding takeaway cappuccinos, sitting cross-legged on checked rugs laid out with variations on hummus and carrot sticks. I see young dads with babies strapped to their chests, staring bleary-eyed into the distance while pushing another child back and forth on a swing. I sometimes see kids crying in the sandpit and their mums squatting to toddler eye level, telling them not to throw sand at their friend. Observing these scenes always gets me reminiscing about my days as a young mother, doing exactly the same things. I'd spend every morning at a local park catching up with mum friends and sharing our common experiences: how much sleep we got the night before, how many steps our children had taken, whether they'd started solids yet or concerns about them having high temperatures. If I wasn't with other new mums, I'd be off on some adventure with my little ones: looking for crabs in rock pools at the beach, drinking babycinos at little cafes we'd walk to, visiting chickens at different houses down the street or watching planes take off through the fence at the airport. We'd always be out somewhere, little sultana boxes in hand.

It's true what they say about how this stage goes so quickly: it seems like yesterday that I was in this phase of my life and, honestly, I loved all of it. But even though I feel warm, fuzzy and nostalgic when I peer out of my car window at these young families who are so early in their parenting journeys, I smile a little and think, yeah, nah, no thanks. I don't want to be doing that again. That's a hard pass for me. Those activities are for that generation now, and I'm supposed to be doing something else. They can have it now. And I continue driving in my car that is baby-seat, nappy-bag and rusk-smeared-pram free.

Developmental psychologists talk about critical periods of development. Well, my critical period for early parenting was about 17 years ago, and all those areas of my brain are now grown over with other stuff now. Granted, a lot of that stuff is still kid-related, but it's now more teenager-related and all that goes with that phase. Conversations about babies' sleeping, toilet and feeding habits ... Well, I think those neural connections have long been pruned away. 'Sorry, I won't be available. I will be travelling in Italy with my handsome young Italian lover,' I declared to my teenage kids recently when they were talking to me about having their own children in a few years and how I could help them out by babysitting. Seeing as I do not have a handsome young Italian lover, my comments were met with laughter, but I was deadly serious: I'm planning on having a break for a few years once they are out in the world by themselves. I don't want to go straight from two decades of looking after kids to looking after more kids. This sounds harsh, but given I can't even resist looking after baby birds that fall out of the sky in front of me, how would I ever say no to a grandchild? Best I warn them now that I will be busy enjoying a Sangiovese watching a dusty sunset across the Tuscan vineyards with young Giovanni.

The overwhelm, anxiety, irritations and crises that can happen on a parenting journey are different for everyone, and so many diverse stories are shared on the psychologist's couch. It might be the sheer overwhelm from the multitude of duties that a parent has to perform on top of working full-time, the anxiety and exhaustion of caring for a newborn, the stress of parenting a neurodivergent child, it might be the painful empathy of a parent watching their teenager break up with their first love, the conflict with a partner about misaligned parenting styles, the fear of co-parenting with a difficult ex-partner or the battles of parenting an adolescent girl who's been leaving the house wearing a skirt that is way too short. Some midlifers are also dealing with the heartbreaking reality that they cannot have children at all, which can take many years to reconcile and accept.

On top of all of this, many midlifers are part of the sandwich generation – those who are who are caring for their ageing parents while also looking after their own children and working. We cannot ignore the significant strain that this dual caregiving role can cause. The 'village' doesn't operate like it used to, and many are lacking a wider support network, so modern parenting in the developed society also means a sheer excess of tasks, duties and roles. This physical and mental load can lead to feelings of overwhelm and, sometimes, burnout.

Whether we had children in our early 20s or are still having them in our 40s, our children change a lot over the course of our middle age. Whether we are ready for it or not, our kids grow up and we grow along with them. Our parental role changes dramatically as our children grow up. We're transitioning to a different type of parenting at each stage and adapting to our kids' requirements of us. Much of our midlife is spent preparing to launch our kids into their own lives, independent and free from our rules and coddling. This is something that not only our children have to get used to, but us too.

For women, midlife parenting often means navigating

puberty and perimenopause at the same time, with all the fun (not) that comes with both. Perhaps there is an evolutionary reason for this? It would make it so much harder for teenagers and young adults to fly the parent-controlled coop if we were all getting along swimmingly. Are we supposed to morph into grumpy ogres just so our children leave the nest? It's not conducive to procreation if our kids 'fail to launch' because we're too soft and cuddly. Is it all so they will be happy to leave? 'Maybe it makes it a little easier if we part ways when I'm at my most difficult, and they're at their most difficult,' laughed one of my teary-eyed clients recently when discussing the mixed emotions that come along with children moving out. 'I was so much nicer when my kids were younger. I hope they remember me from back then.'

Having our children move out after consuming our lives and identities for decades can cause a considerable jolt to the psyche. Upon reflection, many parents find themselves with not only more spare time on their hands, but also what feels like a brain full of solid neural connections now floating around doing not much. Some find themselves asking questions such as, 'Who am I beyond being a parent?' 'How do I define success and fulfilment for myself now that my children are no longer living at home?' 'What parts of my identity have I set aside all these years while raising children, and do I need to revisit them?' These questions may seem discombobulating at the time but can pave the way to a reinvention of self, beyond being a parent.

Empty-nest syndrome is a common experience for midlife parents whose houses were once filled with little kids, then teenagers and young adults, and who are now left feeling the psychological jarring of no longer being at their offspring's beck and call. What was predicted to be a momentous occasion can leave parents feeling lonely and as though something is missing in their now quieter (but often neater) homes. I often talk to parents in midlife about how crucial it is for them to find areas of fulfilment in their lives that are independent of their parenting role. It helps them ease into new roles over time without interfering with their children's developmental needs for greater independence. On the other hand, some parents are excited about their kids flying the nest, but, knowing that they may fly back at some point given the current cost of living, are also thinking, 'Maybe I shouldn't convert their bedroom into my reading sanctuary quite yet.'

But whether we are going with the flow and shouting 'Woo hoo!' about our newfound freedom, or we're resisting the onslaught of change, parenting is an ongoing journey, and the scenes are changing constantly. Every phase is different, and one phase's learnings can be applied to the next phase. But, of course, the older they get, the more children ridicule. One minute your small child is looking at you with loving adulation, so much so that they declare that they want to marry you when they grow up; the next minute they're a teenager having a little chuckle at your outfit, telling you the shoes you have on look like something Captain Cook would wear.

Or maybe that's just me.

Considerations

Are you experiencing any negative feelings in relation to parenting?

What specific challenges have you identified?

What are your strengths in this area?

What specific actions can you take to move towards feeling more content?

Challenge

Spending Quality Time Together

Your relationship with your child can change across your parenting journey, along with your parental role. This can be confusing at times, and lead to miscommunication and sometimes disconnection as we react to these changes. Planning activities and scheduling in time to spend with them one on one (whatever age they are) can allow you to reconnect with your child and strengthen your bond. Start by brainstorming a list of activities both of you enjoy or want to explore, such as cooking, playing sports, or even a weekend away together. Choose a few activities from this list and schedule dedicated times for them in your calendar. Gather the necessary supplies and fully engage in these moments, focusing on active participation and meaningful interaction. After each activity, discuss what you enjoyed and any new insights you gained, making plans together for the next child-parent date!

Commitment

Going forward
I commit to these
new rituals to
help me nurture
my family ...

CHAPTER 11

Learn to Be Only, Not Lonely

'IS HE BETTER than my solitude?' This is the question that I will give as an answer every single time someone tries to set me up on a date. It's never an inquisitive, 'Oh, what's he like?' or, 'Who is it?' or, 'How do you know him?' or even a, 'Who would play him in a movie?' (okay, I have asked that one). It's my serious enquiry as to whether this person, who my friend is thoughtfully trying to connect me with, will be a bonus to my life as it currently stands. The life that is alone in the sense of not having a partner but is otherwise fulfilling. The life that involves spinning a lot of plates in the air, yes, but that I'm also deeply invested in. I ask this question because I don't want my solitude – which I'm quite content with, thank you very much – to be messed up by somebody who is not right for me. I'm never sure if my friends get the drift of what I'm trying to say, because it's never too long before I have to have the same conversation again.

If I was to get a gold star for something in life, it would be being single. I've dabbled with dating here and there in recent years, but after a few lengthy relationships in my younger adulthood, my middle age thus far has been spent mostly alone. And while every day I put 100 per cent effort into my life – my kids, my health, my career etc. – zero effort is invested in finding a partner. This is all much to the chagrin of my friends and family, who find it more difficult than I do that I'm not in a relationship at this stage of my life.

Many people in middle age find themselves alone, whether it is by choice or by accident, and, in contrast to my 'quirky alone' confidence, not everyone is content with it. In fact, it can be quite a distressing state in which to find oneself in midlife. Time and time again, as a psychologist, I see middle-aged people desperately unhappy, thinking that their misery is because they are alone or haven't found their romantic match yet. I have days full of sessions with forlorn clients who, from my observation, need to work on a whole lot more than their dating skills. By pulling the conversation away from their lack of relationships and looking at their lives with a wider lens, we'd be able to do a heap of work together that would lead to a more fulfilling life – with the by-product often being either contentment with solitude or a relationship with someone new. But these are their sessions, so relationships or lack thereof are what I usually must focus on – for a while, at least – until I can sneakily divert them back. People generally put so much effort into finding someone who ticks all the boxes, yearning not only for happiness but security, safety and comfort, that they neglect to try to create these things for themselves first.

This is through no fault of the people I work with. We've all been there. I've been there: upset, sad and even distraught that I'm not coupled up, thinking that everybody around me is in a wonderful relationship and I may as well go and eat some worms. There's no doubt that there is a belief in our society that most of us have grown up with: that being single is something we must fix, and that if we don't currently have a partner we should at least be on the hunt for one. We are told that we will be in a constant state of unfulfilled limbo until we are in a relationship.

But being alone doesn't have to equate to feeling lonely, just as not being alone doesn't equate to not feeling lonely. Being in a relationship with someone doesn't always guarantee you won't feel disconnected, disengaged or just psychologically on a different page from your partner. We can be in a relationship and still feel lonely if there is someone lying right beside us. I hear this all the time.

Middle-aged people's relationship crises often revolve around the fear of being alone. Aloneness is likely to happen at some point in our lives, whether we like it or not. Whether we planned it or not. Whether we remain alone or not. I've heard countless stories from clients over the years who've found it incredibly challenging to be without a significant other. The separated woman who is now panicking that she will be alone forever. The guy who keeps getting told, 'It's not you, it's me.' The single mum who lies in bed between her two children wondering if she'll ever have the time to date again. The 40-year-old who had to move back in with his parents after his separation. The depressed woman who still hasn't found 'the one'. The newly divorced guy who jumps straight into a relationship with the same 'wrong' woman. The unhappily married woman who is too scared to leave for fear of what's on the other side. The widow who is still in the thick of losing 'her person'.

Given we will all have at least a moment or two of being alone on our life's journey, knowing what to do with alone time will be useful. Not only so that we don't nosedive into the depths of psychological distress when it happens, but also so we can learn to push past the initial discomfort of being alone and learn a different way to live that might be beneficial for us going forward.

For myriad reasons, loneliness can start creeping in during middle age. This is why connecting with ourselves and learning to feel content in our own company are so important. When working with clients who are alone (and who are particularly distressed about it), my aim is to ease them into becoming comfortable first. I'm helping them to realise that we can be by ourselves and still have wellbeing. I'm teaching them that we sometimes need time alone to better understand ourselves and who we truly are. The test is to learn to be alone *without* being lonely; it's to connect with all parts of ourselves.

This might mean nurturing our interests by spending more time doing them. It might mean learning to do things we've never done before or trying activities we've never tried before. It might mean prioritising self-care, scheduling it into our diaries because it is as important as any other activity. It might mean joining more groups that share our interests. It might mean getting out more. It might mean reconnecting with people we haven't seen in a long time, who we would have otherwise been too busy to see. It might mean nurturing parts of our lives that may have remained dormant if not for time alone. It might even mean taking a break from social media or getting support to manage our minds to stop comparing ourselves with other people. It might just mean doing *whatever we goddamn want.*

Novelist May Sarton said, 'Loneliness is the poverty of self; solitude is the richness of self.' Being alone is something all of us will experience at some point in our lives, but it certainly doesn't have to feel lonely. Sometimes solitude can be the best thing you ever had. Once you experience it, you never know, you may never want to part with it.

Considerations

Are you experiencing any negative feelings in relation to being alone?

What specific challenges have you identified?

What are your strengths in this area?

What specific actions can you take to move towards feeling more content?

Challenge

Weekend Solo Date

Taking yourself on a solo date can be a refreshing and empowering experience. Set aside a day on a weekend coming up. Write a list of activities that you genuinely enjoy and that bring you joy, whether it's visiting a favourite cafe, creating a vegetable garden, exploring a museum, going to the movies, hiking in nature, or simply reading a good book in a cosy spot in your garden. Allocate the full day, prioritise your preferences and create an itinerary that caters to your personal interests and is just for you. This dedicated time allows you to reconnect with yourself, recharge your energy and appreciate your own company. Reflect on how it felt afterwards and think about how you can bring some of these activities into your daily routine. Having a structured schedule that involves a variety of activities can help you feel more productive and balanced when alone.

Commitment

Going forward
I commit to these
new rituals to help
me learn to connect
with myself and
be comfortable
with being alone
at times ...

CHAPTER 12

Enhance Friendships

I DON'T KNOW why it took me so long to figure this out, but it's possible to go out socialising on a Saturday night *and* still get to bed early. When I realised this was a socially acceptable thing, it was a game changer. For much of my adult life, I've thought an evening out involved ... well, spending most of the actual evening out. My concept of socialising on a Saturday night was formed back in young adulthood, when I was up to all sorts of things with my friends in the middle of the night. But for the last nearly two decades, I have not been going out much because I had kids at home and had to be all mature, dependable and responsible ... things I don't feel like being at times. I've said no to many evening events unless they've been family related and, quite frankly, I became quite accustomed to this. Now my kids are teenagers, so I can leave them at home by themselves while I go out and socialise a little. How, you ask? The key is to start early and finish early. What a revelation! Now, it's a no-brainer: if anyone want to go out for a raging Saturday night with me – a couple of drinks, delectable food and long chats – then it's a 4pm start and

8pm finish, baby. Mama wants to be at home, heels off, bra off, make-up off and in bed in her pyjamas reading her book by 9pm. Gasp in horror at the nanna state of my social life if you want (or maybe deep down you're a bit jealous), but for every gasp I'm sure there's something that resonates.

Saturday night is my night off. It's the one night I'm not sitting in a shopping centre car park waiting to pick up a teenager or driving another teenager home at 9.30pm after sports training. Saturday night is the only night I'm not serving dinner numerous times for different kids around their weeknight commitments. Saturday, despite it still involving an excessive amount of kid-wrangling, life administration, family visiting, work, household duties and whatever else the weekend expects of me, is somewhat slower than the rest of the week and, more to the point, doesn't have tasks that slide into the evening. The evening is all mine. But at the same time, I want that evening to end relatively early because I've always had a busy week (as I'm middle-aged, and we've established quite clearly thus far what that entails). I don't want to be running on an empty tank on a Sunday because a) I don't want exhaustion to wreck what I want to accomplish and b) I don't want exhaustion to wreck my Sunday rest time (if you know what I mean). This is why that 4pm–8pm slot on a Saturday is the Goldilocks position for me at present. And my friends embrace this because it works for their stage in life too. Along with semi-regular lunch dates and sending my friends hilarious dog memes in between, this level of socialising gives me a feeling of social contentment at this stage of my life, and I'm sure it will only get better. It makes me feel excited about retiring one day: I often wonder whether retirement will be when my socialising is at its peak. Is retirement when I will get to hang out with my friends more? Is it when I'll be able to sit in cafes and while away the hours talking about old times? Is it when I'll have long lunches with my girlfriends and not have to worry about rushing back home? If you look around at pubs, cafes, local pools and beaches during the working week, those places are not full of young people socialising, but rather older adults. Something to look forward to.

Often by middle age we find that our social lives have changed along with us. Many of us are not socialising like we did when we were younger, and the people we spend time with are often not the peers who were so heavily part of our lives growing up. Friendships were probably our most important relationships in our teenage years, and as adult responsibilities crept up on us, some of our friendships faded away. It's well established that our social network dwindles across our lifespan. Some people move out of our lives and new people appear. Many middle-aged people report that they don't have as many friends as they used to, and even when they do have friends, they tend not to see them very much. 'We need to catch up soon' is the social catchcry of the middle-ager. We want to catch up, but in our hectic lives, we just forget those intentions as the months or even years go by.

My client Linda echoes this. She was surprised to see a whole heap of friends come out of the proverbial woodwork to support her while she was going through chemotherapy. Having struggled to organise catch-ups or attend their previous 'ladies' lunches' they did long ago when their kids were little, Linda hadn't seen them much at all in recent years. But when they found out about her cancer, they were there in a heartbeat. One joined her for her regular chemo sessions, another caught up with her for weekly lunches and another cooked her dinners to reheat in the evenings, knowing she would be feeling sick and exhausted. Another who was far away rang her every night to debrief on the day. She saw her friends more in those six months than she had in the previous ten years, but now that she's cancer free, her friends have disappeared back to the hustle and bustle of their own lives.

It's not that we don't love our friends anymore; we just haven't had the time needed to nurture our friendships. 'If I have a spare moment in my day, as much as I love my friends, I don't even think to call them. I tend to just sit down and have a cup of tea,' said my client Kate. Every minute of the day seems to be allocated to work, family and household responsibilities. Many middle-aged adults experience a lack of support and connection, with loneliness creeping over them at times, and the lack of time to maintain their friendships is a major factor in this.

Apart from declining unintentionally because we are too busy to maintain them, many friendships naturally dissipate over time. So many significant life events happen during adulthood that by the time we reach middle age, we can have but a handful of friends left. Career changes, relocation, marriage, divorce or parenthood can see friends hopping on and hopping off our friendship train. Some come along for the ride for a little while if they are at similar life stages or we work with them, but few stay for the full journey. We may find comfort, understanding and camaraderie in connecting with others who are like us or who are navigating similar challenges and milestones, but in the stripping away of friendships that have run their course, middle-agers can feel stuck in a kind of friendship limbo. With the wisdom that only comes from living for decades and experiencing friendships with a variety of people, we often start realising we need more out of these relationships, especially since we have less time for socialising. We want these interactions to be positive, fulfilling and real.

In the therapy room I've seen discontent with social lives develop for a variety of reasons. I've seen clients who don't feel fulfilled with their friendships anymore as their values are not in alignment, I've seen some become disillusioned with people they've known for a lifetime because of betrayal. I've seen people who have just been spending time with friends out of habit, rather than for the enjoyment of it. I've seen the sadness that arises from a friendship fading. I've heard about misunderstandings, grudges, conflict, jealousy, lies and distance tearing friendships apart. But discontent can also arise from loneliness, from feeling you have no connection or belonging with others.

Many of my male clients in particular have talked about their lack of friends. They tend to have workmates, but not the deeper level of connection that they truly want. This feeling of seclusion, of being alone, can be exacerbated when their romantic relationship breaks down. Who do they have to properly talk to? Who can they be vulnerable with? Being lonely doesn't sit right with them (even when they won't admit it) and it can heavily impact their mental health and wellbeing, sometimes spiralling into depression. Social support enhances resilience and protects against mental health disorders that can develop through stressful times, and too many middle-aged men are without it.

Being pack animals, human beings fare better when they are socially connected. Social support is one of the most important ingredients in the recipe of a psychologically and physically healthy life. Nurturing friendships is a crucial part of building a longer, happier and more fulfilling life. Being around friends increases the release of several hormones and chemicals in the brain and body including endorphins, dopamine, serotonin and oxytocin (our 'cuddle hormone') which can reduce the physiological effects of stress (lowering cortisol) by helping us feel safer, comforted, valued and needed. Research has even shown that often we are happier around our friends than our family. I'd guess we can all think of a time when we have debriefed with our friends over a cup of tea (or wine) and the weight of our problems has been gently lifted. Friendship also protects us against a host of health conditions, from the common cold through to cardiovascular disease, by improving immunity and reducing inflammation in the body. Research has also shown that a strong support system can help in recovering from cancer and chronic pain, as well as preventing debilitating conditions such as dementia. Social support is associated with lower rate of mortality and morbidity by contributing to better health outcomes.

Moving towards contentment with friends may mean being proactive and checking in with them, even if we're presuming they may be too busy. It's likely they've been thinking exactly the same thing about us. I often talk to my clients about the 'low-hanging-fruit friends'. These are the people who we know already, but haven't connected with properly for a while. We need to ask ourselves how we can reconnect with them. Are there friends from the past that we can reach out to, to rekindle what once was?

However, in many cases, we are just in dire need of new friends. We live in a transient world where we are moving all the time, and we often don't have the 'village' environment in which we grew up, so we have to look for new connections in the communities we now reside in. In pretty much all cases, we're not going to find these future friends by sitting on our couch; we will find them by engaging in our own interests, participating in local activities and exploring new hobbies near where we live. Middle-aged people can break through the bubble of our peers and open ourselves up to a diverse range of people with whom we'd never have thought friendship possible. People of different genders, cultures and ages can reflect to us parts of ourselves that have lain dormant for so long and can make our lives richer than they were before.

Most importantly for a fulfilling middle-aged social life, learn from the first half and take those friends who resonate with your soul along for the ride of the next half. Nurture them along the way. If we put in the effort to know who we are and be more authentic, it's interesting to witness who will jump off and head in the other direction, and who will jump on for the ride.

Considerations

Are you experiencing any negative feelings in relation to your social life?

What specific challenges have you identified?

What are your strengths in this area?

What specific actions can you take to move towards feeling more content with your social life?

Challenge

Join Clubs or Groups

Joining a club or a group is a great way to meet new people and expand your social circle. Start by identifying your interests or hobbies, whether it's sports, arts, volunteering, education or even work-related. Research local organisations, clubs and groups that align with these interests, and reach out to see if you can attend any of their gatherings, events or meetings to get a feel of it. It might be a little uncomfortable at first if you don't know anyone, but engaging in conversations and participating in some capacity may allow you to connect with like-minded individuals – and a bonus may be that you make new friends over time.

Commitment

Going forward
I commit to these
new rituals to
help enhance my
friendships and
become socially
connected ...

CHAPTER 13

Align Professionally

IN THE PAST year or so, after particularly heavy workdays, I've found myself staring out of my car window a little more than I usually do as I wind my way back home slowly through the streets of my suburb. It's almost like I'm catching up on the day that was happening in the outside world while I was caught up indoors: elderly people walking their dogs around the lake, couples sitting in cafes, kids running around at football training and people pulling into their driveways after work. Like the garden voyeur that I am, I take particular notice of gardeners at work, pulling weeds, raking leaves, cutting trees and mowing lawns. And I catch myself thinking, 'Look at them, working outside all day in people's gardens in the fresh air and sun, walking up and down, up and down, up and down ... That looks like such a good job. I wouldn't mind doing that.'

When I'm not thinking about opening a lawnmowing business, I'm often thinking of opening a plant store, or a gift shop, or a small bar. I can sit on a career move or a business idea for months. 'Hmmm, maybe a small bar with books lining the walls so people can sit and read quietly with a glass of wine,' I'll delusionally tell a friend. 'Or maybe it won't have any books; I'll just make it so the environment is conducive to deep conversation and connection, so people can debrief about their day. Maybe I will call it … Wine & Whine.'

Other times my mind takes me in an entirely different direction, entertaining the idea of buying an old house in some quiet seaside town and spending my days renovating it. Perhaps I would Airbnb it when I finished it, or maybe it would just be for me, to sit and write all day, staring out at the ocean.

One would think that after having studied for so many years to become credentialed as a psychologist, I'd be established enough in my career to have cruise control on for the rest of my working life. One would also think that after all that hard work at university, which has only started to pay off recently, I would not be pondering entirely different careers. I've been a psychologist for a while now, and my entertaining other interests, jobs, businesses or even whole careers doesn't mean I don't enjoy my profession; it's more about recognising that I only have one life, and thinking that perhaps I should do something different in the second half of it. I've been a psychologist – should I try something else now? To quote Mary Oliver, what else can I do in this 'one wild and precious life'?

In recent years, in my midlife, this line of thinking has become stronger than ever. I'm not alone in feeling like this. Many people I have worked with feel a little psychologically itchy about their careers in middle age. Many burst out of high school a few decades earlier and landed themselves any job they could find, and after many years they are now wondering whether it's time for a change. Others jumped onto a socially dictated pathway early on, studying for a degree or other qualification because it seemed good at the time (to a pimple-faced teenager with no life experience anyway) or because they were persuaded to by a parent. Now many are at a crossroads at their halfway point in life, thinking that this isn't what they ever really wanted to do, and that perhaps it's time for a change. Other middle-aged individuals are now in a position to cut down work hours, or even to go back to work after raising family. For those who haven't worked for years, this can be a time of upheaval, disruption and anxiety (how times have changed if you've had 15 years out of the workplace). Whatever the case, middle age can bring on a feeling of confusion about one's vocation. I still wonder at times ... what will I be when I grow up?

Many of my past clients who are in a state of career crisis are those who have succumbed to burnout or are on the pathway to it. Burnout is a psychological syndrome that develops in response to prolonged exposure to chronic stressors. It's a state of mental, emotional and physical exhaustion that emerges because an individual's nervous system is continually on alert, as though they are constantly under threat. Burnout was included in the World

Health Organization's 11th revision of the International Classification of Diseases (ICD-11) in 2019 as a purely occupational phenomenon. It is described as 'a syndrome conceptualized as resulting from chronic workplace stress that has not been successfully managed'. Holistic psychologists like me know that one facet of a person's life cannot be treated in isolation from the others, and that burnout is not solely caused by our occupation – but work is often a major factor.

In my deep conversations with burnt-out clients, we delve into areas of their work lives that could be causing the build-up of chronic stress and the distress that follows. Tales of difficult colleagues, ineffective leadership, boredom, unrealistic expectations, no recognition, overwork, unsupportive management and unhealthy systems come up time and time again. Burnout is an unwelcome disruption that often occurs in midlife, but after recovery it can become a catalyst for career change that we didn't realise we needed. The crisis that is career burnout stirs something inside us and becomes a wake-up call to start thinking about what work, job or career we want to be doing going forward. It can prompt the reflective time needed to tweak our work role, to communicate our needs to management or to set boundaries with colleagues. Sometimes it's the push to quit and find a job that better aligns with who we are on a deeper level, to retrain for something that we always wanted to do or to go out on a limb and open our own business.

By midlife, we're often a bit exhausted and weary of the working world, but we have a lot of experience under our belts, and a lot of ideas about how work can be done better. 'I just can't do people anymore,' opined one of my coaching clients recently. Mel is a people and culture manager and has been working in human resources with 'people' for too long, it seems. But after much soul-searching, Mel started her own consultancy business, which allowed her to avoid getting caught up in the politics of people so much. Middle age brings about these kinds of reflections on things that aren't working in our careers. The unhappiness at work. The frustration of dealing with poor management. The regret of not having done things we once wanted to do. The realisation that we've been working too hard for too long. The culture of 'hustling'. The lack of fulfilment. The people ...

We needed these experiences – the good and bad, the work-related and people-related – to gain some wisdom for our future. Bottle this wisdom up as a midlifer and you'll have the motivation to make good career choices for the next half of life. There are questions that start creeping into the midlife psyche, such as, 'If not now, when?' I've had midlife clients from the corporate world becoming executive coaches, hospital orderlies becoming nurses, lawyers becoming house renovators, teachers becoming entrepreneurs and doctors becoming gin distillers. There might even be a psychologist opening a small bar in the future. Who knows?

Despite the challenges, some people at middle age are at the top of their game career-wise, with a wealth of experience in their field that can only be gained over many years of work. Contrary to what we might see on social media, many of the most successful people in the world didn't achieve their success until after age 40. Their experience (which includes making mistakes) and wisdom equipped them with valuable skills, insights and knowledge that contributed to their success in their careers. This is true of historical figures such as Leonardo da Vinci, who completed some of his most famous works, including the *Mona Lisa* and *The Last Supper*, during his 40s and 50s. William Shakespeare wrote some of his most celebrated plays, such as *Macbeth* and *King Lear*, around the same age. In more recent times, well-known figures who had spent most of their early lives working away with little recognition only came to prominence after their 40s. Vera Wang began her career as a figure skater and fashion editor before transitioning to fashion design in her 40s. Samuel L Jackson was relatively unknown until his breakout role in *Pulp Fiction* at the age of 46. Louise Hay didn't publish her first book, *Heal Your Body*, until she was 50 years old. Nobel and Pulitzer Prize winning author Toni Morrison, Marvel legend Stan Lee, home and kitchen icon Martha Stewart, award-winning actor Betty White ... Need I go on?

For most people, the wisdom that we need to decide what we want to do when we grow up ironically takes *years* to develop, whether it's through experience on the job, building extensive professional networks or becoming more financially stable. This wisdom is what helps us to know that, deep down, we do (or don't) want to be doing our jobs anymore. This all takes time.

Might see you at my bar or while I'm mowing your neighbour's lawn.

Considerations

Are you experiencing any negative feelings in relation to your career or vocation?

What specific challenges have you identified?

What are your strengths in this area?

What specific actions can you take to move towards feeling more content?

Challenge

Your Ideal Workday

Taking some time to imagine your ideal workday is a great way to reflect on whether your current work life aligns with what you truly want to be doing, and helps you start actualising what you truly want to be doing. Begin by envisioning your perfect morning routine: what time do you wake up, and what activities set a positive tone for the day? Think about how you can align this routine with your strengths and values. For instance, if you're energised by a structured start, maybe you plan a short workout or meditation session before diving into work. As you outline your workday, consider the tasks and projects that make you feel most fulfilled. How can you structure your day to focus on these strengths and passions? What will you be working on? Who will you be working with? What environment will you be working in? Finally, wrap up your day by thinking about how you unwind and recharge. Write this all down in a journal in fine detail. To make this ideal workday reality, identify the key changes needed in your routine, work environment or job responsibilities to align with your vision. Set some key goals for yourself so you can work towards transforming your current workday into the perfect one you've envisioned.

Commitment

Going forward
I commit to these
new rituals to help
me align myself
professionally in
work or vocation ...

CHAPTER 14

Engage in Joyful Activities

RECENTLY I'VE DISCOVERED an interesting fact about magpies. Did you know that if a magpie's beak is mostly white, it is an adult bird, older than two years of age? Magpies who have a half-black and half-white beak are adult birds, but likely under two years of age. Those with a black beak are the young birds. Fascinating, isn't it? I'm no naturalist but it's nice to know facts about nature – though this one does have practical application in my life given the magpie family that lives near me. When I'm on the veranda writing and they bounce over to me in their feathery tuxedos, heads titled to the side as they give me an inquisitive little bird side eye, it pleases me to know whether they are a baby or an older, wiser magpie who knows where it's at.

I love animals, and there's never been in a time in my life in which I've not had pets in the house. The 'nature child' in me needs to be nurturing some animal, it seems. I've had dogs, cats, mice and rabbits, but I've never had a pet bird. I prefer to enjoy them flying around in their natural habitat rather than confined to a cage. But though I don't choose to have a *pet* bird, I often tend to have *a* bird.

Being the avid walker that I am, I'll inevitably stumble on some sort of bird that is sick or injured and in need of assistance. It's not uncommon for me to be walking home with dog leash in one hand, bird wrapped in a jumper in the other, my shredded fingers in need of a dousing in antiseptic. I don't choose birds, but birds choose me – I've had doves, pigeons, cockatoos, galahs and magpies. As I write this, I have a rainbow lorikeet with a broken wing in residence, who I found dazed by the side of a busy road.

My dad is a similar manifester of wounded birds. Even though we never had pet birds growing up, we'd always be caring for an injured bird that he had found by the side of the road. We'd walk into the bathroom of our family home and there would be a feathery fluff ball staring up at us, perched on a branch balanced over the bathtub, which would be lined with old newspaper. Us kids would research what that kind of bird ate, try to replicate its habitat so it wouldn't be too psychologically affected by the trauma (I started early) and carefully look after it while it healed, until eventually we'd release it back into the sky with Dad at the local park. And here I am in my own adult life, buying berries, melons and expensive hanging seed bars and wandering the neighbourhood like a crazy bird lady looking for plants and flowers that my bird of the month needs for rehabilitation. The apple never falls far from the tree – or, in our case, the bird.

I was reading a news article recently that talked about

how, as we get older, we start having more interest in birds. From memory, it was something of a piss-take article about the signs of ageing, but nevertheless it resonated. And by the looks of the people in the bird-group photos I often see in the community newspapers, it's likely true that it's mostly older people who are into 'birding'. But on a more serious note, I'm finding that as I get older, I have a yearning to do new things, explore other interests, look outside of what I do every day and step out of the usual busyness that seems to dictate my life. I want to participate in new activities, gain more knowledge about fascinating topics and explore new areas of life, for no obvious reason. Just because I want to. I'm starting to daydream about what I could do next just for the pure enjoyment of it, and contemplating where on my Google Calendar it will be scheduled.

This is something I'm noticing in my middle-aged clients too. They're reflecting on what they have been spending their time doing in adulthood and whether they want to continue the same way with the same routine for the rest of their lives. In a lot of my coaching sessions, my corporate clients – who have spent a good chunk of their life studying and working, and squeezing in caregiving duties around those things – are starting to wonder whether all their hard work, all their career focus, all of the missing out on other parts of life, has been worth it. Now, with the wisdom of hindsight, there is a slow realisation that they are moving past the halfway point of their life and that there may be more to it than just working and caregiving. It's often something they haven't thought about before. Sometimes, a little panic sets in as they ask themselves, 'Have I been working too much? Have I been spending enough time with people I love? Have I been doing anything I just want to do for the pure joy of it?' Many people who are facing death in old age report realising that what they once thought was important doesn't matter much in the long run. A recurring theme is that they now use their time to engage in activities that are pleasurable to them – something midlifers operating in high gear don't tend to prioritise. This can teach us to live more meaningful lives and the beauty of middle age is that we can apply this lesson now, way before we reach old age.

Some middle-agers feel financially settled enough not to work as much as they once did, some are clawing back a little more time as their children grow up, and some just think, what the heck, I need more 'me time' in my life. Some middle-agers start revisiting their childhood passions and dreams, some start entertaining new activities that have sparked their interest and some start becoming more curious and begin trying new things to see what might light them up.

I often ask my clients who are unhappy, overwhelmed or feel like there is something missing in their lives whether they ever do anything just for fun. They usually just stare blankly back at me. They haven't got time for fun, and if they did, they certainly wouldn't know what to do with it. 'I don't even have time to pick my nose,' my client Julie responded to this question, laughing. To give my clients ideas for activities that don't involve earning an income, getting something finished or achieved, or whatever other important outcome us adults seem to value, I often ask, 'What did you love doing when you were younger?' Thinking about what we did in earlier periods of life, just for the intrinsic enjoyment of it, can give us some information about what might be missing now. Many of us got caught up in what life said we *should* be doing, rather than what we really wanted to do. Good on those who manage to follow their dream and live their passion; but for many of us, some parts of our dreams didn't quite get realised, or maybe some parts just got forgotten. Many of us have a life within us that is still sitting there, waiting to be lived. Perhaps we naturally leaned towards these areas in our childhood, but life just took us off on another pathway. But at midlife, reflecting on these old passions can get us thinking about what might need to come back into our lives now. For some people, having passion in anything is long forgotten, and they have no idea how to find it again now. That's where curiosity comes in: trying, attempting and testing life in different ways to see if something sparks inside you. This might mean learning a new skill, experimenting with innovative recipes, immersing yourself in unfamiliar book genres, travelling to different places, trying new sports, attending cultural events, enrolling in fascinating courses, started interesting projects, adopting new routines or even redecorating your home.

To keep ourselves happy and healthy in middle age and beyond, we need to find and practise activities that we enjoy. We need to claw back our time by scheduling joyful activities into our diaries and communicating this to those around us. We need to insert what gives us pleasure into our schedule as though it is as important as a meeting or an appointment . We need to be playful in the moment, with no strings attached. We need to dust off the piano, unzip the surfboard from its bag, enrol in that art class, take that golf lesson or even begin a newfound hobby of 'birding'.

Considerations

Are you experiencing any negative feelings in relation to time spent on enjoyable personal activities?

What specific challenges have you identified?

What are your strengths in this area?

What specific actions can you take to move towards feeling more content?

Challenge

Regular 'Joy Breaks'

It's often hard to find time for hobbies and other extracurricular activities in our busy schedules, so proactively scheduling them in can balance out our day. To incorporate joyful activity into your day, try scheduling a 'Joy Break' where you intentionally engage in something that brings you happiness. This could be anything from taking a short walk in nature, enjoying a favourite hobby such as painting, surfing, cooking, gardening or playing a musical instrument, or spending time with someone special. Set aside 15–30 minutes specifically for this activity, and fully immerse yourself in it. By making this a regular part of your routine, you can boost your mood and add a sense of joy to your daily life. Additionally, you can keep a 'Joy List' of activities that make you happy and rotate through them to keep things fresh and engaging. Prioritise this chunk of time daily and make sure it is treated as important as appointments, meetings and other daily tasks.

Commitment

Going forward
I commit to these
new rituals to
help me prioritise
engaging in joyful
activities ...

CHAPTER 15

Find Solace

IF IT WAS me instead of you reading this book and I was up to this chapter on death, I would probably skip it and just go on to the next chapter. 'Yeah, I'll come back to this later,' I would say, convincing myself that I'd read it another time because it's an important chapter to read, but I probably don't want to get myself all upset right now. But deep down I would know I never would.

For the last decade or so, I have noticed that I use this death discussion avoidance technique in my personal life. I skip episodes of TV shows where I suspect a character might pass away, and I completely avoid movies where I know someone is likely to die in the end. When I was younger, I would leave the cinema sobbing, crying in the car on the way home with my family: *The NeverEnding Story*, *Beaches*, *Steel Magnolias* ... Oh my gosh, and *Ghost*. I grew up, like many kids in the 80s, watching the most traumatic movies for entertainment. They seemed to almost always end in someone unexpectedly dying, something that we were not prepared for as we innocently walked into the cinema holding our popcorn and choc bombs.

Of course, with baby boomer parents at the helm, there was no debriefing afterwards to help us reconcile what we had just watched. I remember watching *Watership Down* as a 'fun' end-of-year movie in *grade two*. Those movies hit hard back in the 80s, and you'd think that those of us who grew up in that era would be psychologically inoculated against the deaths of people we know and love in adulthood, but I'm not so sure. All I know is that I've experienced a couple of decades of non-fiction adulthood since then, in which many people in my life have passed away, and I can no longer be entertained by fictional deaths. Today, if I start watching a movie and get even a whiff of an impending protagonist death, it swiftly gets replaced with an Adam Sandler comedy. We all know they're safe.

Death is a funny thing. It's funny because it isn't funny at all, yet *we* are funny about it. It's something that will happen to all of us, and eventually it will happen to everyone we know and love. But we avoid it. We talk about it for a while after it happens, and then we just start to change the subject. But we lose people around us with ever-increasing frequency as we age, and it's something that can't be skipped or avoided. The impact of a loved one's departure can be literally life changing. As Haruki Murakami writes in *Norwegian Wood*, 'Death is not the opposite of life but an innate part of it.' By middle age, this feels all too true. It's something that we need to learn to tackle head-on, as it is a part of life and isn't going to go away.

Death has had such a profound effect on me as a midlifer, probably more than anything else. Just when I feel as though I can't deal with the effects of another death, another one comes along. Like many midlifers, if it's not someone I know personally or professionally who's died, it's someone who I feel has been part of my life, but in an unrequited way. We only have to turn on the TV or open our newsfeeds in the morning to see that someone we idolised, someone we follow, someone whose music we danced to with our friends as a child and whose lyrics we knew every single word of, has left us overnight. Just like that. Despite my sadness about the loss of such legacy-leaving public figures, and my nostalgia about the part they played in my life, when this happens I pragmatically think to myself, 'Geez, we don't get long on Earth, do we?'

That's the psychological motivator that I draw out of death: among the heartbreaking distress that loss can elicit in us, it's a reminder that we don't get that long to be alive. I'm not going to write the clichéd statements about grief that we have all heard or, in sympathy, offered to those in the midst of deep sorrow, even though more often than not these are true. Grief is such a deeply personal experience that we need to sit in it for a while, wade in the emotional depths of it (whatever that looks like for us) in our own timeframe, and eventually find our own meaning from it. Then, when we're ready and have dusted ourselves off, we can apply this meaning to our own life. Yes, for those of us who are left behind, life does go on, but it's always different from what came before.

In bereavement research, this is known as 'dual process' coping. We can grieve by mourning our losses, staring teary-eyed out the window for a few weeks in the depths of sadness or even punching a few doors in our anger that they are no longer here. We might try to get on with things but be in a robot-like state of denial, or even distract ourselves for a while to avoid the pain. We might linger in a state of longing for them to return, yearning for how things were. But however we feel our feelings after a loss, running psychologically parallel to all of this is a restoration of sorts: we create a new normal day by day, engaging in old and new daily activities and making new plans. The loss of people we were close to does change our lives, and we have to adapt accordingly by reinventing ourselves to realign to life without them. It's okay to oscillate between processing the trauma of losing someone and renewing ourselves. If we get stuck in one of these processes and don't go through the other, we can either jump into a new life too quickly without processing the grief enough to learn the deep lessons we need for truly renewing ourselves, or we can remain stagnant, bathed in negative emotions.

I'm well versed in the loss of loved ones and I still don't know what to do with the feeling of loss at times. Processing grief is a deeply personal and individual journey, and there is no one-size-fits-all approach to dealing with it. How I grieve is different to how someone else grieves. Even as a psychologist, I can't teach people how to grieve – I've just got to meet people wherever they are. I've got to let happen what needs to happen for them, in the safest and most supported way possible. Even if you get your grieving process 'perfect', whatever that looks like, the next time will be different, I can assure you of that. Personally, some losses I can make sense of, some I can't; some I can talk about, some I will change the subject on quickly; some I know I will never get over, some I can reconcile because I can tell myself it was their time; and some, well, I still don't know what to do with them because it's just too hard, so I've placed them in the 'too-sad basket'. Sometimes among the loss you can find something a little funny as you sit in the nostalgia of the memories of your loved one. 'She loved cake,' said my friend with a tear-stained face a few years ago as we stood under dark umbrellas in the rain at her grandmother's funeral, after she had scraped a slice of strawberry torte off her plate onto the coffin that had just moments before been lowered into the grave.

I've spent hours and hours in private practice helping people navigate grief. I've noticed that early middle-agers tend to not quite have a grip on it yet, particularly when death is new to them. They don't know what to do with it, where to put it, which emotions to let in or who around them can help them with it. Elderly clients tend to be better at grief; they have an acceptance of it that their younger counterparts don't quite have yet, and although they feel the same depths of emotions, they seem to be able to reconcile the inevitable better than middle-agers can. Life has inoculated them against death many times over, and they have enough evidence to prove that life, even decades later, does indeed go on. They themselves are proof of it.

Death is inevitable, but many of us struggle to make sense of it. Middle age can be a pivotal moment when we start experiencing life that's been impacted by death. As we wade through our experiences of people around us dying, we can either stay in the distress of it all or we can start reflecting more and applying the wisdom that the feelings of loss can bring. One of my middle-aged clients recently told me that he wasn't scared of the 'dirt bed' himself but was bloody well sure he was going to live life to the fullest since his best mate passed away. He committed to living the life that his mate didn't get a chance to. And he certainly did, not only changing some of his unhealthy ways to give himself some energy back, but also embracing a more 'stuff it' attitude and writing a bucket list his mate would have been proud of. My client had evidence that death can sneak up at any time, and he was determined to make the most of whatever time he had left.

We can't help but start thinking of our own mortality when people die, and death is sometimes the shake-up we didn't think we needed. Without it we might continue to sleepwalk our way through life, not spending our valuable days doing what we truly want to be doing in the brief life we are given. Death makes you think about living. If you reflect on death deeply, it can help you to stop sweating the small stuff, prioritise what matters and realise what's missing in your life. It can tell you what to let go of, what needs to move to the top of the to-do list and what needs to slide down (or be kicked off). Death is the shove we need to get healthier, to slow down, to spend more time with family, to say sorry, to forgive, to say I love you, to leave an unhappy situation, to speak our minds, to set boundaries and to really know what matters. Death can make us get a wriggle on with our goals and our dreams, giving us the kick up the butt we didn't know we needed.

The eighth and final stage of Erik Erikson's theory of psychosocial development, which I mentioned in chapter 7, is 'integrity versus despair', a psychosocial crisis that people in late adulthood battle. Old age is when we tend to look back at our whole life, think deeply about our accomplishments and regrets and reflect on the meaning of our life. If we evaluate our life and conclude that we lived it with meaning and purpose, we can sit back in our armchair with a cup of tea and feel a sense of integrity. If we evaluate ourselves as not having lived with meaning or purpose, a deep sense of regret and despair can intrude upon us. Reflecting in middle age and learning from death, seeking wisdom in loss and applying that to our life, gives us the chance to change course earlier in our journey before it's too late. This is an important part of the seventh stage, 'generativity versus stagnation'. Losing people around you can give you a chance to evaluate your life, putting you on a better path sooner rather than later. There will be the deaths of others, but at the same time, if you allow it, there will be the renewing of you. As death researcher and psychiatrist Elisabeth Kübler-Ross and David Kessler wrote in *On Grief and Grieving*, 'The reality is that you will grieve forever. You will not "get over" the loss of a loved one; you will learn to live with it. You will heal, and you will rebuild yourself around the loss you have suffered. You will be whole again, but you will never be the same. Nor should you be the same, nor would you want to.'

The death of people around us is part and parcel of being alive. Even if we're lucky enough to have escaped it earlier on in our lives, death inevitably starts appearing in middle age. As much as I would love to, there's no skipping this chapter of life – or of this book. But to move to the acceptance state of grief, we must first feel the emotions that will arise from loss and, in good time, tap into the wisdom that it gives us.

Considerations

Are you experiencing any negative feelings in relation to loss or grief?

What specific challenges have you identified?

What are your strengths in this area?

What specific actions can you take to move towards feeling more content?

Challenge

Creative Expression

Engaging in some sort of creative expression can be a powerful way to process and navigate grief. Creative activities such as art, music or writing a letter can provide an outlet for your emotions. Consider starting a personal creative project that reflects your feelings and memories of your loved one. It might be painting because that helps you express how you're feeling, it might be creating a playlist of music you once enjoyed together that will draw out those emotions you may have been holding on to, or it might be writing in a journal to help you express how you feel in words. Creative expression can help you process your grief in a therapeutic way, so you can find a sense of solace over time.

Commitment

Going forward
I commit to these
new rituals to help
myself find solace
in the loss I have
experienced ...

CHAPTER 16

Achieve Inner Peace

AS I'VE MENTIONED, I like to walk a lot. Rain, hail or shine, you will find me wandering around, gazing at cloud formations, checking out birds in trees, chatting away to my dog or merely daydreaming. Whatever the weather, I will be out walking. I draw the line at lightning, of course, as one needs to be safe and sensible as a middle-aged person, but I will literally weather a storm if it falls during my 'walkies' time. Occasionally, depending on what I have on the agenda, I will have a bonus walk in the middle of the day; I take any opportunity I can get to be outside in the fresh air and moving. Winter walks are my favourite, with the cooler weather allowing me to linger longer outside, enjoying the heat that my body creates through physical exertion. On hot summer days, I tend to bookend the day by moving my long walks to before sunrise and after sunset, maintaining my nature time but sensibly escaping the scorching Western Australian heat (and preventing any paw-pad sizzle for my trusty walking companion).

I walk to stay physically active, to keep fit, to spend time with my dog and to suck up everything nature has to offer.

I feel healthier after moving my body, absorbing sunlight, listening to birds chattering and breathing fresh air. I also walk to create that much-needed third space away from home and work, to process my day and to have a break from the tasks I likely spend too much time immersed in. I feel more relaxed, recharged and less stressed when I'm walking. I also walk to think, to ponder and to wonder. I feel as though it gives me more clarity of mind and makes me more productive at work. I'm so disciplined with walking that when I get invited to a work or social event that lands during my scheduled walking times, I feel a little bit of panic come over me at the thought of missing out on my walk. I'll answer a reluctant 'yes' while simultaneously scrolling through my calendar to see what time I can shift my walk to.

I get so much benefit out of my daily walks that I can't imagine ever getting to a place in my life where I'm not partaking in them. Nelson Mandela stated that the world would be a better place if we prioritised education and equal opportunities for all, the Dalai Lama said it would take looking after our environment and natural resources, and Helen Keller thought social justice could only be achieved if we all took responsibility for our actions and their impact on others, but I strongly believe that the world would be a better place if we all took a long walk at either end of the day.

I find another interesting phenomenon occurs when I'm walking, a bonus that I had never predicted until I experienced it. It seems that in the act of moving outside in nature, unplugging myself from my computer, my phone and my excessive daily to-do list and removing all the other hats I wear during the day, I can connect to something deeper. It's a wordless state of oneness that puts me on a different frequency than I was on before, a sort of zoning out. I'm not quite sure if I'm tapping into something internal or external. Whatever the case, I believe this is where some sort of magic happens for me: deeper processing occurs, reinterpretation of the day happens, learning solidifies, dots connect, perspectives change and always, always, ideas come rushing. And this is a little bit addictive. There are some days where I head off on a morning walk along the coast, into bush parklands or even through the tree-lined alleyways of my suburb and feel the urge to just keep walking, with the only thing stopping me being the wretched timer that pulls me back down to alert me to what society expects of me that day.

I feel that this type of spiritual connection has crept up on me as I've moved into middle age. I don't recall feeling like this at earlier times of my life. I wasn't so cognisant of my need for peace, silence, reflection and connection until recently. Until midlife. Perhaps when we are children it happens quite naturally, but it simply gets lost along the way once we get older and become immersed in the bustle of the external world. We start listening to the loud shallowness of society and stop listening to the quiet depths of something bigger than ourselves. And now, as I start clawing back a few more moments of time to myself as a midlifer, I can hear something else that's been silent for a little too long. Or maybe it was there all along and I just couldn't hear it. Maybe I needed to get to middle age to take notice. Maybe I needed to undertake decades of life, experiencing tough times, becoming alert to my own mortality and realising that there are likely more years behind me than in front of me to take a few spare moments of the day to listen. As spiritual teacher and Buddhist philosopher Thích Nhất Hạnh explains, 'At any moment, you have a choice, that either leads you closer to your spirit or further away from it.' It's only when you take the time to stop and listen that you get the information you need to create what's next.

I'm not alone in my sentiment here – many midlifers slowly realise that something is missing, then search for something spiritual to tap into; something bigger that's outside themselves, yet very much inside themselves at the same time. Often, they don't know what that is, but it exists outside of their daily routine, outside of the many hats they wear and outside of what society has been telling them. Even some of the seemingly most cognitively rigid people I've worked with seem to be more open to spiritual exploration once they start creeping into their fourth decade and beyond, with years' worth of life behind them. This openness usually sits in juxtaposition to an existential dread that wasn't there before. Sometimes the uncomfortable latter has to raise its ugly head first to thrust the former into action. Without the angst, without the internal dialogue of 'What's this all about?' 'Is this it?' or 'Who even am I?' we would likely just keep sleepwalking through life. Which is exactly what many people do. Spiritual teacher Marianne Williamson sums this up in her book *A Return to Love*: 'It takes courage ... to endure the sharp pains of self-discovery rather than choose to take the dull pain of unconsciousness that would last the rest of our lives.'

In the midlifers I've worked with, the calling to become more spiritual doesn't always manifest the same way. Contrary to what people might think about spirituality, it's not necessarily about locking into a particular religion. It's a broad and deeply personal concept that encompasses beliefs, values, practices and experiences, and is related to the deeper aspects of life. When people become more spiritual, they are on their own individual (or collective) search for meaning, purpose, connection and transcendence beyond the material world that they are so familiar with. To some, this might be 'God', another divine being or even their higher self. Other people tap into 'the universe' or 'the source'. It doesn't really matter what it is. As author Julia Cameron writes, 'You do not need to work to become spiritual. You *are* spiritual; you need only to remember that fact. Spirit is within you.' For me, spirituality is faceless, wordless, with a feeling of oneness that warms me. It's not grounded in any religion, but time seems to stop when

I tap into it (well, until my alarm goes off). I can rarely access it when I'm drinking a prosecco and eating tapas with my girlfriends, and it certainly doesn't happen when I'm scrolling Instagram. I'm definitely not in that stream of consciousness when writing emails or organising my taxes. I'm way too much in my own head to have room for anything spiritual in those moments (particularly with my taxes).

In many cases with midlifers, the calling to become more spiritual comes from a place of distress, chaos, discontent or even crisis. Not only wanting to shift the negative emotions that they can't seem to shake and soothe their soul, they are often searching for bigger answers about why such terrible things can happen in life, whether it be a relationship breakdown, a health diagnosis, a loved one passing or even all of these things in a short amount of time. It's not uncommon for people to look outside of what they are familiar with in the physical realm and search for answers elsewhere. To quote Ted, my client who recently went through a series of unfortunate events in quick succession, 'I'm not religious or anything, but is there some spiritual guru out there somewhere who can give me a straight answer about why all this shit keeps happening to me? Have you got any recommendations on some good books?'

I've steered many of my clients who have gone through difficulties in midlife in the direction of books, as that is where I too have found solace and made sense of life's challenging moments. Whether it's Eckhart Tolle, Wayne Dyer, Gabrielle Bernstein, Marianne Williamson, Deepak Chopra or Thích Nhất Hạnh, absorbing their wisdom and philosophies can give us a way of making sense of what is happening to us. And once we settle on a particular philosophy and gain some peace from it, we can find a practice or two to ritualise in our lives – something we can draw upon, again and again. For some it might be meditation, mindfulness or repeating mantras. For others it might be praying to archangels or just lingering a little longer in the meditation part of their weekly yoga session (that part always feels so good you want it to last forever).

Some people, at middle-age crisis point, return to what they once did to connect with themselves when they were younger – maybe something they did as a family but stopped in early adulthood, almost as a passive rebellion against their parents. This might be an organised religion, or it might be tapping into the oneness they once found in nature. Others are finding their spirituality for the first time in middle age. I have endless conversations with clients who have previously relegated practices such as meditation to the woo-woo section of bookstores where they dare not go, who are now organising meditation retreat weekends in the forest. They cannot do without it.

For others, finding peace and connection in a more traditional spiritual sense is all a bit too freaky, and to suggest something too enlightening, such as sound therapy, is pushing it (as a therapist, I can see this when clients' eyes start glazing over). I can tell they are yearning for the same peace, to connect with something outside of themselves, but they prefer to connect to the present moment using some form of activity. Taking a walk in the park, hiking in bushlands, joining a beach dippers club or connecting with nature in other ways can nourish their soul and deepen their sense of connection to something greater than themselves. Many spend time outside in their once-neglected gardens or the gardens they once paid others to tend to, finding connection there among the fresh air, trees and bees.

Several people I know have also connected spiritually through volunteering and service, not just connecting with something outside of themselves but fostering their sense of interconnectedness with others. Others have explored creative outlets such as art, music, writing or dance as a means of self-expression, connecting with the inner child who once did all these activities for no other reason but pure enjoyment. These are activities that we did when we allowed our true self, rather than society, to tell us what we 'should' be doing at any moment.

Like many people I work with, I didn't really feel that I needed a spiritual connection and nor did I search for one until I was older – after I had experienced decades of life and gone through a fair chunk of adversities. It wasn't until I had searched for happiness in the wrong places that I realised I need to look elsewhere. This is what living life does:

it gives you the years and the experiences (good and sometimes downright awful) necessary to find a deeper meaning to life. And we've lived a lot of life by the time we get to middle age. We needed to wade in the shallows first to realise that there is something more important somewhere. And what's there is not necessarily what we thought it would be; it's a deeper meaning, purpose and significance in life.

Whether we call it spirituality or not, middle-agers often start becoming more aware of ourselves – and start wondering why we are here at this place and this time. Midlife can be a time of connecting with our inner wisdom, intuition and higher selves, and developing a deeper understanding of ourselves and our place in the world. We are trying to attune an antenna that can help us find our way into our next phase. With the realisation that we are closer to death than we are to birth, sometimes a spiritual panic can come over us, making us wonder if we have got it wrong so far and whether we can turn that around.

Like me, many of my clients are on a quest for inner peace and fulfilment. They have a heightened awareness of the limitations of material success and external achievements in fostering lasting happiness and fulfilment. When I was younger, I spent so much time bringing material 'things' into my life, but now I spend more time taking 'things' out. I don't want them as much anymore. Many middle-agers are seeking experiences that transcend all of this. Some have experienced material wealth and thought, 'So what? This stuff isn't making me happy. The external validation I so desperately craved is not what it's cracked up to be.' The striving, hustling and seeking of achievement slowly starts to wear off, and in its place we seek peace of mind and calmness. So do we keep being busy like society tells us to be, or do we stop, connect and listen? The silence is where our spirit is going to tell us what we really need and start guiding us there.

As author Neale Donald Walsch explains, 'The deepest secret is that life is not a process of discovery, but a process of creation. You are not discovering yourself but creating yourself anew. Seek therefore, not to find out Who You Are, but seek to determine Who You Want to Be.'

I'm finding my next phase in life on my walks – where are you finding yours?

Considerations

Are you experiencing any negative feelings in relation to spirituality or finding peace?

What specific challenges have you identified?

What are your strengths in this area?

What specific actions can you take to move towards feeling more content?

Challenge

Meditation Ritual

Meditation is a powerful tool to assist you to find inner peace. To find inner peace through meditation, start by creating a calm and inviting space, perhaps with a candle or soothing music. Set a clear intention for your practice, such as finding tranquillity or releasing stress. Get comfortable in a seated or lying position, close your eyes and take a few deep breaths. Perform a slow body scan, relaxing any areas of tension, and then focus on your breath, visualising calmness with each inhale and letting go of tension with each exhale. Use a calming mantra or affirmation, such as 'I am at peace,' to centre your mind. Visualise a serene place, such as a peaceful beach or quiet forest, immersing yourself in its tranquillity. Embrace the stillness, express gratitude for the time you've taken, and gently transition back to the present by wiggling your fingers and toes, stretching, and opening your eyes. Carry the sense of peace with you throughout your day.

Commitment

Going forward
I commit to these
new rituals to
help me achieve
inner peace ...

CHAPTER 17

Address
Global Crisis

I WAS HAVING a discussion with my teenagers recently about kids' perceptions of their parents. It was around Mother's Day and the obligatory social media posts about beautiful mothers and how special they are were in full flight. But among the perfect mama tributes are always my favourite posts: when honest mums showcase their little ones' portraits of them that they created at school. In these pieces of artistic gold, you will likely see a more accurate portrayal of mums – triangle skirt over stick legs, scraggly hair, drinking wine with some swear words in a speech bubble floating up in the air (always with gigantic eyelashes, of course). 'My mum's favourite activity is ...' asks the half-completed worksheet from the teacher. 'dRinKing wIne,' writes the child. I find these posts so humorous, maybe because as a psychologist, what I know to be true of people is often not what they portray to the outside world. Sometimes asking our children what they honestly think of us can hold a mirror up and tell us something interesting about ourselves that we hadn't even noticed. And perhaps that honesty is the first step in growth.

So just for fun, I asked my kids to tell me what they think about me. 'What do I spend my time doing?' 'What do I say a lot?' 'What are my favourite things?' I asked. They came up with a whole heap of observations such as 'You work hard,' 'You walk the dog a lot,' 'You eat lots of vegetables,' 'You look nice when you're on TV,' 'You look after us,' etc., which are all valid, I guess (even if I only seem to look nice when I'm on TV, which is for a total of three minutes a week). But what I found interesting is that they also mentioned, 'You say "honestly" a lot.' When I pressed them about it, they said that I say it all the time, like as in an exasperated '*honestly*' accompanied by a shaking of the head and sometimes an eye roll. And, yeah, they're right. I probably say this numerous times a day. It's usually issued in reaction to what is happening in and around me because it beggars belief. 'Honestly' is an all-encompassing word that I use to express a range of emotions in a socially acceptable manner. I tend to use 'honestly' when my kids are fighting, when I'm reading ridiculous commentary and stories on social media, but mostly I use it when I'm watching tragic world events on the news. It's a word that covers many fleeting feelings, but at the same time I use it to internalise way too many negative emotions such as anger, frustration, sadness and disappointment. If I were to break down my 'honestly' reaction, I'd find a cluster of feelings that I'm holding within me. These emotions are important pieces of information that need to be listened to.

The world is a strange place to live in right now. As a midlifer, I'm not sure I like it that much at times. Just look at what's going on in the world around us – *honestly*. Every day it seems we wake up to headlines informing us of more atrocities in the world, heart-wrenching news that leaves us in tears, feeling uncertain and disappointed in the world we live in. It seems as though a day doesn't go by without a reminder of how frightening the world can be, whether it be from crime, war, violence or another type of injustice. And given we have devices at our fingertips at all times, we are constantly witnessing this and, with throbbing empathy, feeling the emotions that go with it.

I often wonder whether our ancestors felt these feelings of stress, uncertainty and fear in the same way that we feel them now, or whether the time it took to relay news back home and the lack of visual connection to global events facilitated a cognitive dissonance for them. Was there a separation of sorts, a barrier to them thinking too deeply about what was going on in the world in order to prevent their own mental discomfort? Perhaps our relatives had a gestalt view of wars and other atrocities, and unless they personally knew anyone in their family or their hometown who was affected, they could keep a psychologically safe distance from it all? Of course, our relatives would have been dealing with a harsh and complicated world as much as we are now, plus their own individual adversities – an even harder life, perhaps. Maybe there was more of an acceptance of the uncertainties (and certainties) of life back then, and a feeling of powerlessness that came from having less choice and less control over parts of their lives. I wonder if midlifers back then thought like we do now. I wonder if the people in their 40s back in 1945 felt too that the world was falling apart when their husbands, brothers and sons did not come back from the war. I wonder whether my British relatives thought about the damage to the environment from pollution when they walked home from work in thick black 'pea soup' fog. Or was everyone just too busy focusing on their own basic needs? As Abraham Maslow suggested in his work on humans' hierarchy of needs, it's hard to prioritise facilitating a sense of belonging in your town, working on your own career, falling in love or reaching your potential if you don't have food, water, warmth, shelter or security. Fighting for survival would have been a priority for most of our ancestors rather than finding the time to self-actualise.

I don't remember a time in which there wasn't a global atrocity happening; in 2024 we're absorbing the traumas of Gaza, Ukraine and Sudan, among hundreds of others. When I was younger, it was the Vietnam War and the Gulf War. I remember my grandfather talking (rarely) about his role in World War II as a gunner on the back of a British warship; I could listen to those stories with a sort of naive disconnection because it felt like they belonged in the distant past. But looking back now, I realise these horrors would have occurred only 40 years prior to the conversations I was having with my pop. It had only recently happened, and for those who survived it, the memories were still very much alive in their minds. Whether it was the stories of the regimes of Adolf Hitler, Joseph Stalin, Mao Zedong or Pol Pot or the hundreds of others that my Western history textbooks did not teach me about, these atrocities are part of modern history. For midlifers now, it would be like these things happened in the last 40 years. It's hard to fathom for some of us, but no so hard for others, as it was and is reality for them and their loved ones. Not everyone in Australia has the privilege of being removed from global atrocities. It is still very much happening now. It feels like a world that only our ancestors went through. If we are not living through it, we can still feel psychologically removed from it, only being affected if we step into the stories (which many people can). Back in my pop's era adults would read about war developments well after they happened. They'd perhaps hear about them on the radio or in the newspaper days if not weeks after the events occurred. Given television wasn't introduced into Australia until the late 1950s, people were certainly not seeing moving pictures of the atrocities while sitting on their couch in their living room day after day. While some historians suggest that humans have been destroying each other since the beginning of time, others argue that society is much less violent than it used to be and that, compared to the cruelties of wars in centuries past, we are living in the most peaceful era in history. Whatever the reality, it's devastating to witness so much violence.

As a middle-aged person living in the current world, it feels as though we've been coping with endless world crises in the last few years, mainly caused by our fellow human beings. We can watch the world's traumas and tragedies unfold in real time, which not long ago would have been reported days, if not weeks, later keeping us somewhat at arm's length and mentally disconnected from them. Perhaps in the past, human brains were able to reconcile the events as if they were fiction. With the 24-hour news cycle, our minds are now absorbing these atrocities while we're having our coffees in the morning, while we're eating sushi for lunch and as soon as our heads hit the pillow. In the past, people had only poor-quality black-and-white imagery, and things would have been quite sanitised for home audiences. Now we are able to access high-quality imagery and firsthand accounts of traumas and tragedies directly from the source through social media, often without even a warning that we are about to see graphic content. Sometimes it's literally unfolding in real time as a livestream.

I'm sure I'm not the only one who makes a pact not to watch the news again, but then can't even last a day without doing so. It's always a choice for us to not read, watch or listen to the news. We don't have to absorb what is going on. But we still do, and we still should. It's crucial that we know about current events in order to understand the world around us. It allows us to be informed citizens, which helps us to navigate our life. It educates us, gives us perspective and helps us understand people around us. As disappointing and distressing as what we are witnessing can be, and as worrying as it can be that our world is playing out like this, we can still do something with the feelings that go with it. But we must be vigilant about how the news impacts us – it can cause us to sink into despair by leaving us with a skewed outlook on life, particularly if we are obsessively viewing distressing content. I talk to clients all the time about the anxiety they feel about what's going on in the world; they might feel helpless, powerless or even depressed about what they are viewing, reading about or hearing. I often tell people that if they find themselves feeling like this, it is important that they take steps to put their mind at ease, first and foremost. If they are mentally in a place of fear, they are not going to be able to make a difference, make a wrong right, stand up for what they believe in or start fighting for a cause, whether it's on an individual or more collective scale. I urge them to think about what they need around them to nurture their wellbeing, to surround themselves with people they connect with and partake in activities that make them feel secure and safe. Looking inwards and making sure that we are okay first allows us to foster the psychological capabilities to handle what's not okay externally.

At middle age, with growing morality, rising confidence

and a brewing sense of injustice about what's going on in the world, along with increasing wisdom, people often start thinking of the difference they can make in society, the wrongs they can help make right and the legacy they can start building to make the world a better place. Middle age is where I've seen more people standing up for their rights, fighting for important issues, marching in rallies, donating to causes, inspiring others to make change and cutting down their paid jobs to volunteer for charities. Midlife kicks off a sense of purpose outside of ourselves, outside of our home and outside of our usual roles.

The world can be a little disappointing at times, and it can feel volatile and uncertain, but that doesn't have to stop us from creating some good news for ourselves and our fellow human beings. And what an important realisation to have in middle age ... *honestly*.

Considerations

Are you experiencing any negative feelings in relation to the crises that are happening across the globe?

What specific challenges have you identified?

What are your strengths in this area?

What specific actions can you take to move towards feeling more content?

Challenge

Community Action

It can be distressing to witness the injustices that are happening in our world, but we can use our emotions as a call to take action and make a difference. Think about a particular cause that is on your mind and close to your heart. Spend some time researching what people around the globe are doing to help with the cause. Think about the realistic amount of time, resources and capabilities (no matter how much or how little) you have to contribute, either globally or locally. This could involve volunteering with local organisations addressing a particular cause or crisis, participating in online forums to share resources and strategies, supporting advocacy groups working on solutions, raising money, or even starting your own charity or group. By actively contributing to efforts, whether through direct action, raising awareness or supporting those in need, you can create a sense of agency and connection and make an enormous difference.

Commitment

Going forward
I commit to these
new rituals to
help causes close
to my heart ...

CHAPTER 18

Reconcile the Past

'I DIDN'T REALISE he was such a handsome man,' I silently thought to myself. 'Why did I never notice that before?' Here's me, lying in bed one night, after falling down the YouTube rabbit hole watching old Fleetwood Mac concerts. Not sure how I ended up there – I obviously clicked on a music video that piqued my interest at some point in my scrolling – but there I was, hours later, lost in the music of my childhood. Music from our past seems able to elicit feelings in us that are quite different from what the music of today does. While we can turn on our radio now or pop on a playlist and enjoy newly released music for what it is, it doesn't give us the nostalgia, those sentimental feelings we have for former times in our life. And there's nothing like music to get one reminiscing about the past: 'Uptown Girl' playing on the record player at home, 'Thriller' at the skating rink with primary-school friends, 'Vogue' with high-school mates in dance class and 'Come On Eileen' on the nightclub dance floor after a few too many. These are memories from long ago that make me smile. Granted, I may have forgotten what Lindsey Buckingham and the rest of his band looked like when they were young, or how handsome Lindsey was. I was probably busy playing with my Barbie when Fleetwood Mac was at the height of success. But nevertheless, their music, and that of many other musicians of that time, filled the air of my childhood. Listening to it today still has the power to bring me comfort.

My mid-50s client Lynne once asked me, 'Is it normal that I spend hours watching old music concerts? I watched a great Rolling Stones one last night. Have you seen that one?' Well, too much of anything can be a bad thing, and we don't want to be dwelling on our past at the expense of the present; but once we got talking more about it, we worked out that Lynne's habit wasn't excessive. Relishing in the memories of old music videos seems to be a common pastime for middle-aged adults. If it's not on YouTube, it's a music documentary on Netflix or, for those who are a bit more tech savvy, a nostalgic back catalogue of music on TikTok. Once those algorithmic tentacles get hold of you, there's no end to it – your device will be delivering you Hall & Oates videos for hours.

But nostalgia does not come only from listening to music. All our senses can evoke it. It can come from our childhood photos, a particular flavour, a conversation with a friend about school days or even the smell of a particular aftershave. A taste, a smell or a sight can give us a feeling of times long past. Nostalgia brings up the emotions we attach to memories of people we've met, places we've been and events we've experienced. Sometimes the feeling is so positive, so wistful that we long to return to that time. The reason why nostalgia feels so good to us is that our primal brains at an unconscious level don't know the difference between a thought and reality. So if we're revisiting happy times in our minds, our bodies react as though it's happening now. The part of the brain that holds our memories lies right next to the part that controls our emotions. That's why we cry, laugh or just give a sly little smirk to ourselves when we reminisce about what we got up to in the past. The bonus nostalgia gives us is that we usually won't remember every fine detail about the memory. So we remember our moves on the dance floor, not the hangover the next day. We remember the Calvin Klein aftershave, but maybe not so much the guy.

Nostalgia's role is to give us a taste of sentimentality, the feelings we had in that moment. We all get nostalgic from time to time, but maybe we should be doing it more often. I often spend time talking to my middle-aged clients about their past, asking them what they were like when they were younger, what their homes were like, what they spent their time doing and what their interests were decades ago, long before they sat in my office. When people are going through difficult times in the present or even experiencing some sort of identity crisis, they can find themselves stuck in reminiscent conversations, lost somewhere in their memories. Other times, nostalgia can reinforce our sense of identity by reminding us of our personal history and experiences – especially if we're thinking about what made us happy in the past, just for the sake of it. Other times, nostalgia can reinforce our sense of identity by reminding us of our personal history and experiences as we reflect on what we used to do that made us feel happy.

Studies have suggested that we're more prone to nostalgia during difficult times and that nostalgia reminds us of the possibility of better days ahead. In fact, research suggests that feelings of nostalgia increased during Covid-19 quarantines, serving as a comfort during isolating times. Reminiscing about the past has been shown to help us feel connected to who we were in the past, who we are in the present and who we will be in the future, helping to promote a sense of self. Reflecting on past achievements and the overcoming of obstacles can bolster our confidence and motivation to get through present difficulties and remind us of the resilience we have within us. We remember what we did before when life was difficult, and what we did to get through it. By rummaging through old photo albums and memorabilia, I've had clients remember that they used to take regular dance classes, that they spent every weekend surfing with their mates, that they holidayed regularly in beach shacks up north, that they spent hours fishing, that they had dreams to write books, and how talented they were at drawing back in school. These little clues about who they once were can be a source of inspiration in middle age and a friendly reminder about what can be tapped into to create what's next.

To be clear, when we talk about nostalgia, we're talking about the good memories – but talking about the past doesn't always deliver feelings of nostalgia. It can be quite the opposite. So many of us mental health professionals have spoken with clients who are still depressed or anxious or in some other sort of distress due to past experiences. Past experiences shape our beliefs, behaviours, experiences, identities and feelings. Some of our memories are considerably hard to bring up, so much so that we never do. Yet they are often silently affecting us, consciously or unconsciously prodding us to make certain decisions, behave in certain ways or even head in certain directions. By the time we settle into middle age, we've racked up a few decades of life experiences, some of which have been quite challenging. But with the negativity bias that unconsciously guides our minds, the more difficult moments of our life can dominate. Fear will often triumph over fearlessness. Sadness will cloud happiness. Resentment will devour forgiveness. Guilt will eat relief for dinner. Our brains will hold onto every memory that elicited a strong negative emotion in the past, all in the name of protecting us in the future. But unfortunately the future is now, and at middle age we might still be feeling the same emotions, not letting go of things that need to be released, holding fast to outdated beliefs and limiting our lives because of it. The comfort zone that we have created by holding onto the past can begin to feel uncomfortable, particularly when we think about how long we might have left. This thinking is often the catalyst for getting help – to start talking about those psychological injuries, to finally process them and leave those memories where they need to stay: in the past.

It isn't only the big traumatic experiences that have the potential to knock us off axis in our first half of life. It can also be mini traumas or moments that seemed insignificant or even normal at the time: the way our parents treated us, our cultural background, schoolyard experiences, our own past mistakes and failures, relationship breakdowns and ex-partners, sicknesses and losses. Our mind holds onto all these experiences in some shape or form, playing a role in who we are today. Us psychologists listen to thousands of human stories over our careers and witness many light-bulb moments in our sessions as we work like detectives to uncover why people are the way they are. There's excitement in the aha moment that comes when the mystery is solved, and then relief. When the unconscious becomes conscious, we can embark on the journey of changing to something that works better for us. Some of the ways we used to operate unconsciously worked for us back then, but they might not be working for us now. And unfortunately, they could be impacting our wellbeing in middle age. Traumatic events from the past can have long-lasting effects on mental and emotional wellbeing. Processing and healing from old wounds often requires acknowledging and understanding how these past experiences continue to impact the present, and it's from here that we can make more conscious choices to design what's next in life. Memories are our internal biographies, and we can tap into their wisdom at any time. Yes, sometimes we will need some tissues handy, a friend to laugh with and a psychologist to help us process it. Sometimes we need to call our parents to make sure we got our story correct and other times we need to write a letter to someone who has passed away so we can accept their death and let them go.

Our past is our story thus far, and it is full of valuable information that gives us clues about who we are and why we might be the way we are. Uncovering this information gives us the chance to change things, do things differently, accept what was, forgive what happened or even let things go. It can also show how strong we are, how good we are at certain things and even who we truly are. Revelling in nostalgia can help us align with who we want to be in the future. Delving into the past in middle age gives us the hindsight that we often wish for ... And sometimes, putting on an old song might be the way to get there.

Fleetwood Mac, anyone?

Considerations

Are you experiencing any negative feelings in relation to your past?

What specific challenges have you identified?

What are your strengths in this area?

What specific actions can you take to move towards feeling more content?

Challenge

Memory Lane

Relishing in our past can give us some valuable information about what we need in the present. Consider a walk down memory lane by creating an experience for yourself that involves revisiting meaningful moments from your past. Gather old photographs, keepsakes, letters or mementos that remind you of positive times and experiences in your past. Allocate some time alone or with friends or family so you can reflect on the emotions and memories they will bring back. You might want to listen to music that was significant for you during those times or play a movie in the background that holds special memories. Immerse yourself in those old times and allow the emotions to rush into the present moment. Reflection can bring comfort and a sense of continuity, and may spark some ideas for you to bring into your life now.

Commitment

Going forward
I commit to these
new rituals to
help me learn
from the past ...

CHAPTER 19

Onwards

I REALLY CAN'T stand reality shows. I don't enjoy them and therefore don't watch them. Maybe over the years they've gotten better and I'm inadvertently missing out on some life-changing champagne entertainment in the evening – I don't know. Over 20 years ago when reality shows took over the prime-time TV spots that beloved sitcoms once held onto tightly, like millions of people I settled in to watch their first seasons. I was never that engaged or excited, even in those early days of what we shall loosely call 'reality' TV. And then, one of my friends entered as a contestant on a show (we won't mention any names). I saw firsthand how unrealistic, heavily produced and unethically edited this show really was, reinforcing everything I already thought. So I haven't watched any ever since. Yes, I get it: people watch reality shows to unwind after a hard day's work, and all of us like to see a bit of camaraderie and competition among people for entertainment. And of course we love the drama. Like armchair scientists we get to watch subjects in controlled environments: small spaces, no sunlight, excessive pressures and a psychopath thrown in for good measure. We watch as these participants get to their most exhausted stages, revealing their dark sides for all to see, the unravelling that happens while being pushed past their limits. That's often what viewers are watching for, if they're honest. There's nothing like a bit of escapism at the end of the day. Okay, yes, maybe I do unnecessarily overcomplicate things a little too much, and as my 17-year-old daughter regularly reminds me, 'It's just not that deep, bruh.' Perhaps it's really not.

But of the plethora of reasons as to why I prefer a book over a *Bachelor* episode, a long walk over a fake wedding, or cooking slowly over cooking to a deadline, is that everything is just too rushed in these shows. Everything involves stress. Everything involves competition, hustling, deadlines, timers, stopwatches, panic and ... drama. It involves the melodramatic 'The world is going to end if I don't get a) the prize, b) the guy, c) the money, d) married, e) the choreography right, f) to arrive at the destination first, or g) the dish plated up in time.' And I don't want any of it. I already need to be quick in my own personal and professional life every day, so I discreetly abstain from it of an evening, rejecting anything that is operating at high speed. I want to be doing the opposite of what these shows are telling me. And this feeling is stronger than ever now as I move through midlife.

As Thích Nhất Hạnh said, 'Many of us have been running all our lives. Practice stopping.' This is what I want.

This is what I'm consciously choosing to do now. After what seems a lifetime (or half a lifetime) of competition, hustling, deadlines, timers, stopwatches, panic and drama, I want to put my brakes on. I want to start meandering in a life direction where I'm slowing down, thinking more, savouring moments and actually smelling the roses. I want to stroll through life and breathe it in. I want to potter around my kitchen crushing fresh spices in a mortar and pestle, making mouth-watering dishes. I want to saunter along the coast having in-depth conversations on long dates with someone, to understand who they truly are before I make any decisions about them. I want to drift around islands on holidays and drink in the scenery. I don't want to run or rush anymore ... I did it way too much in the first half of my life. And wherever I'm going in the second half, I don't care if anyone beats me to it. I will get there eventually, and I will be taking it all in as I go.

Midlife for me is about trying to find more moments of connection to myself – so that I can reflect on my life so far and what I've learned from the abundance of experiences I have had. I'm not going to find the valuable information I need to create what's next in moments of crisis, nor am I going to find it in moments of rushing. The lessons for me come from experiencing the messiest moments and then reflecting on the learnings in the quiet times afterwards. Surely this is how we grow.

~

Middle age is our chance to do things differently. The irritation, the aches and pains, the regrets, the feelings of WTF – these are pieces of valuable information that are telling us what is working and what isn't. And when we move towards creating what will work, then we will be calmer, more confident and, of course, more content. Middle age is a window of time that most of our ancestors didn't have the chance to experience; even now, despite modern medicine, many people we know might never get to, either. It's a privilege reserved only for some. Despite the resistance we may feel initially at its onset, middle age is the second chance we didn't think we needed. It's our second act. Our story is only just beginning.

Slow down, listen to what middle age is telling you, and then use it wisely.

PART 3
Midlife Review

Monthly Midlife Review

Date: _____

Focus areas: Which areas have I identified that might be in 'crisis' and that I should prioritise this month?

- ○ Emotional wellbeing
- ○ Healthy thinking
- ○ Physical health
- ○ Love & relationships
- ○ Parenting & family
- ○ Solitude

- ○ Friends & social
- ○ Career & vocation
- ○ Hobbies & play
- ○ Grief & loss
- ○ Global issues
- ○ The past

Goals: What do I want to achieve this month in these areas so I'm moving towards contentment?

Why: Why do these goals matter to me?

Actions: What micro steps do I need to take to achieve these goals? (Be as specific as you can, e.g. the behaviour, when you will do it, how much you will do, etc.)

1.
2.
3.
4.
5.

Help: List any people you need support from, clubs/ organisations you need to join, appointments you need to make or resources you need to get hold of to achieve these goals.

Reward: Write down a reward you can give yourself if you achieve these goals.

Wisdom affirmation: Write some words you will live by this month.

Reflections: Journal about how you went this month, what your achievements were, what your roadblocks were, what new changes need to happen and what wisdom you could give yourself for next month to move towards contentment.

Acknowledgements

Thank you to my agent, Simone Landes, who has helped me to actualise another book idea (of the many I throw at her) which I hope will resonate with readers. Immense gratitude to my wonderful Affirm Press publishing team; Kelly Doust, Elizabeth Robinson-Griffith, Ariane Ryan, Alistair Trapnell; editors Armelle Davies, Brooke Lyons, and everybody else that worked so hard to bring this book to life and help me share it with the world.

Thank you to my family and friends for their support and for endlessly listening to me waffle on about the next book I'm writing. In particular, a big shoutout to my fellow midlifer friends who I regularly share a wine with, a dinner with or a walk with – all of whom are riding the waves of middle age right alongside me. And thank you to my wonderful clients, who share their vulnerable stories with me, and teach me so much about what so many people in society are really thinking and feeling right now.

On the home front, my beautiful kids, Lali and Luca, who provide me with endless material and also get the privilege (not) of listening to my unsolicited advice every day. And of course big loves to the fur babies who are always by my side when I'm writing and there for endless pats when I'm procrasta-writing ... Chilly, Spooky & Biscoff.

References

Introduction
Kirkey, S. (2020). Forty-seven is the saddest age of all, study finds: 'there is a unhappiness curve'. National Post. https://nationalpost.com/health/health-and-wellness/forty-seven-is-the-saddest-age-of-all-study-finds-hill-shaped-unhappiness-curve-is-to-blame

Judd, B. (2020). 'Middle age misery' peaks at 47.2 years of age – but do the statistics ring true? ABC News. https://www.abc.net.au/news/2020-01-15/middle-age-misery-peaks-at-47.2-midlife-crisis/11866110

Chapter 2
Blanchflower, D.G. (2021). Is happiness U-shaped everywhere? Age and subjective well-being in 145 countries. Journal of Population Economics, 34, 575–624. https://doi.org/10.1007/s00148-020-00797-z

Strenger, C., & Ruttenberg, A. (2008). The Existential Necessity of Midlife Change. Harvard Business Review, https://hbr.org/2008/02/the-existential-necessity-of-midlife-change

Cohen, P. (2012). In Our Prime. The fascinating history and promising future of middle age. Scribner.

Chapter 3
Crimmins, E.M. (2015). Lifespan and Healthspan: Past, Present, and Promise. The Gerontologist, 55, 6, 901–911 https://doi.org/10.1093/geront/gnv130

Chapter 5

Seligman, M. (2002). Authentic Happiness. Penguin.

Gilbert, E.(2006). Eat, Pray, Love. Penguin.

Chapter 6

Gondek, D., Bernardi, L., McElroy, E. et al.(2024). Why do Middle-Aged Adults Report Worse Mental Health and Wellbeing than Younger Adults? An Exploratory Network Analysis of the Swiss Household Panel Data. Applied Research Quality Life. https://doi.org/10.1007/s11482-024-10274-4

Doyle, G. (2020). Untamed. The Dial Press.

Chapter 7

Erikson E.H. 1994. Identity and the Life Cycle. WW Norton.

Chapter 8

Australian Institute of Health and Welfare
https://www.aihw.gov.au/reports-data/health-conditions-disability-deaths/life-expectancy-deaths/overview

Wettstein, M., Park, R., Kornadt, A. E., Wurm, S., Ram, N., & Gerstorf, D. (2024). Postponing old age: Evidence for historical change toward a later perceived onset of old age. Psychology and Aging, 39, 5, 526–541. https://doi.org/10.1037/pag0000812

Ramar K, Malhotra RK, Carden KA, et al. (2021). Sleep is essential to health: an American Academy of Sleep Medicine position statement. Journal of Clinical Sleep Medicine, 17,10, 2115–2119.

Balter, L.J.T., & Axelsson, J. (2024). Sleep and subjective age: protect your sleep if you want to feel young. Proceedings of the Royal Society B; 29120240171

Chapter 9

Australian Bureau of Statistics (2023). Marriages and Divorces, Australia, ABS Website, accessed 22 August 2024.

Brown, S.L., & Wright, M.R. (2019). Divorce Attitudes Among Older Adults: Two Decades of Change. Journal of Family Issues, 40, 8.

Chapter 12

English, T., & Carstensen, L.L. (2014). Selective Narrowing of Social Networks Across Adulthood is Associated with Improved Emotional Experience in Daily Life. International Journal of Behavioural Development, 38, 2, 195-202.

Acoba, E.F. (2024). Social support and mental health: the mediating role of perceived stress. Frontiers in Psychology, 15, https://doi.org/10.3389/fpsyg.2024.1330720

Rico-Uribe LA, Caballero FF, Olaya B, Tobiasz-Adamczyk B, Koskinen S, Leonardi M, et al. (2016) Loneliness, Social Networks, and Health: A Cross-Sectional Study in Three Countries. PLoS ONE, 11, 1: e0145264. https://doi.org/10.1371/journal.pone.0145264

Pasek M, Suchocka L, Gąsior K. (2021). Model of Social Support for Patients Treated for Cancer. Cancers, 13,19 :4786. https://doi.org/10.3390/cancers13194786

Reblin M, & Uchino, BN. (2008). Social and emotional support and its implication for health. Current Opinion in Psychiatry, 21, 2, 201-5. doi: 10.1097/YCO.0b013e3
282f3ad89.

Chapter 13

The World Health Organisation (WHO). (2019). ICD-11: International Classification of Diseases for Mortality and Morbidity Statistics. WHO.

Chapter 15

Murakami, H. (2000). Norwegian Wood. Vintage International.

Barrouillet, P. (2011). Dual-process theories and cognitive development: Advances and Challenges. Developmental Review, 31, 2-3, 79-85.

Kubler-Ross, E., & Kessler, D, (2005). On Grief and Grieving. Simon and Schuster.

Chapter 16

Williamson, M. (1992). Return to Love: Reflections on the Principles of "a Course in Miracles." Harper Collins.

Chapter 18

Weiss KJ, Dube AR. (2021). What Ever Happened to Nostalgia (the Diagnosis)? Journal of Nervous & Mental Disease, 209,9, 622-627. doi: 10.1097/NMD.0000000000001349. PMID: 34448733.

Hong, E.K., Sedikides, C., & Wildschut, T. (2021). Nostalgia strengthens global self-continuity through holistic thinking. Cognition & Emotion, 35,4 730-737. doi: 10.1080/02699931.2020.1862064. Epub 2020 Dec 24. PMID: 33356840.

Newman, D.B., Sachs, M.E., Stone, A. A., & Schwarz, N. (2020). Nostalgia and well-being in daily life: An ecological validity perspective. Journal of Personality and Social Psycholology, 118, 2, 325-347. doi: 10.1037/pspp0000236. Epub 2019 Jan 21. PMID: 30667254; PMCID: PMC7513922.

Chapter 19

Lattin, D. (1997). Stop Running, Start Being. https://plumvillage.org/about/thich-nhat-hanh/interviews-with-thich-nhat-hanh/san-francisco-chronicle-sunday-interview-october-12-1997